—THE—
LITTLE
RED BOOK
—OF—
WISDOM

UPDATED AND EXPANDED EDITION

MARK DEMOSS

The Little Red Book of Wisdom

© 2007, 2011, 2023 Mark DeMoss

Published in Nashville, Tennessee, by Nelson Books, an imprint of Thomas Nelson. Nelson Books and Thomas Nelson are registered trademarks of HarperCollins Christian Publishing, Inc.

Published in association with the literary agency of Wolgemuth & Associates.

Thomas Nelson titles may be purchased in bulk for educational, business, fundraising, or sales promotional use. For information, please e-mail SpecialMarkets@ThomasNelson.com.

Scripture quotations marked ESV are taken from the ESV® Bible (The Holy Bible, English Standard Version®). Copyright © 2001 by Crossway, a publishing ministry of Good News Publishers. Used by permission. All rights reserved.

Scripture quotations marked KJV are taken from the King James Version. Public domain.

Scripture quotations marked THE MESSAGE are taken from THE MESSAGE. Copyright © 1993, 2002, 2018 by Eugene H. Peterson. Used by permission of NavPress. All rights reserved. Represented by Tyndale House Publishers, Inc.

Scripture quotations marked NASB are taken from the New American Standard Bible® (NASB). Copyright © 1960, 1962, 1963, 1968, 1971, 1972, 1973, 1975, 1977, 1995 by The Lockman Foundation. Used by permission. www.lockman.org

Scripture quotations marked NIV are taken from The Holy Bible, New International Version®, NIV®. Copyright © 1973, 1978, 1984, 2011 by Biblica, Inc.® Used by permission of Zondervan. All rights reserved worldwide. www.Zondervan.com. The "NIV" and "New International Version" are trademarks registered in the United States Patent and Trademark Office by Biblica, Inc.®

Scripture quotations marked NKJV are taken from the New King James Version®. Copyright © 1982 by Thomas Nelson. Used by permission. All rights reserved.

Any internet addresses, phone numbers, or company or product information printed in this book are offered as a resource and are not intended in any way to be or to imply an endorsement by Thomas Nelson, nor does Thomas Nelson vouch for the existence, content, or services of these sites, phone numbers, companies, or products beyond the life of this book.

Author photo: Ben Rollins

ISBN 978-1-4003-3695-1 (softcover)
ISBN 978-1-4003-3696-8 (eBook)
ISBN 978-1-4003-3697-5 (audiobook)

Library of Congress Control Number: 2022952470

Printed in the United States of America
23 24 25 26 27 LBC 5 4 3 2 1

He who finds a wife finds a good thing
and obtains favor from the LORD.

—Proverbs 18:22 (ESV)

Children are a gift of the LORD.

—Psalm 127:3 (NASB)

I dedicate this book to the most important people in the world, to April, my wife of thirty-five years, to our three grown children—Georgia, Mookie, and Madison—and to our grandchildren, Rett, Foster, George, Grace, Mary Brooklyn, and our newest due this year. If wisdom is a journey, and it is, I'm privileged to be on it with you.

The world's library shelves are buckled under with books on marriage, and this is not another one. This is a book on wisdom dedicated, firstly, to April, the woman I was somehow wise enough to marry. In her I see the beauty of serving with no motive but to serve. Because of her I know that together we can accomplish more than either of us could in twice the time alone. Alongside her, I've learned to live what matters.

For my years with April, because of April, I am a better and wiser man.

My passion for this book all along has run on the double tracks of wanting to thank my father for how he equipped me and to give my children (and now my grandchildren) the same timeless tools. Looking in both directions, I have the best seat. I admire who my father was, and I sit in wonder at who my children and their children have become and are becoming.

Georgia, always wise beyond your years. I marvel at your maturity, your gentle spirit, your love for others. As a wife and a mother to three boys, your touch is near perfect.

Mookie, even as a youngster you showed wisdom. Your daily practice of reading a chapter from the book of Proverbs plays out now in your marriage and in all you do.

Madison, you stole my heart as a baby, and just to think of you brings a smile. Too few people greet every new day as an adventure and a gift, but you do. Seeing you serve your husband and pour life into your two precious girls blesses my soul.

With every generation the world changes, but life's surest principles never do. In the strong winds of our days, if I could offer you all one anchor, it would be to know and love the Source of Wisdom.

After that, just keep loving each other. My pride in each of you overflows my heart.

Contents

PART TWO: WISDOM FOR YOUR PERSONAL LIFE

CONTENTS

A Matter of Death and Life
Life Is Brief

No one can confidently say that he
will still be living tomorrow.
—Euripides

The entire summer before my senior year in high school I was home for only a few days because I was selling books door-to-door for the Southwestern Company. My father wanted me to do it, and my father was my hero. I agreed to the job not knowing it would mean thirteen-hour days for ten weeks straight, with no breaks even to see my family.

I hated being away from home. I hated missing the weeklong vacation in the Caribbean with my parents and my six brothers and sisters. Every weekend Dad and I spoke by phone—he took great interest in my progress—but a long-distance phone call was no substitute for being with him.

I was back by late August, just before school started. On a Friday, Dad and I met for lunch at the National Liberty

Corporation, the life insurance company he founded and guided to considerable success. I was proud to be his son, proud to walk with him through National Liberty's beautiful home office. Over lunch he and I talked about my plans for college and possibly for business later on.

The next day, Saturday, September 1, 1979, an ambulance sped to our home, where my father had been playing tennis with three other men. One of them rushed to the house to make the emergency call. I didn't think to worry. Plenty of men fall out of breath during exercise. Dad was fifty-three, in the prime of life. I expected to see him in a few hours, back at home with a prescription for heart medicine and a doctor's orders to take it easy.

Instead, my mother and brothers and sisters and I stood in the emergency room of the Bryn Mawr Hospital to hear a doctor say, "I'm sorry. We did all we could." My father was dead, my hero gone. At age forty, with no warning, my mother was a widow with seven children from ages eight to twenty-one. Of course I had known people who died. But I was young. Death happened to older people, in other families.

Shortly after we got home from the hospital that afternoon, my mother found a piece of paper on Dad's nightstand. He was a prolific note taker, never without pad and pen. I can still see the words in his handwriting: *So teach us to number our days, that we may present to You a heart of wisdom*" (Psalm 90:12 NASB).

Arthur S. DeMoss was the wisest man I knew. Now he was in heaven, less surprised by his departure, I suspect, than we were. More than forty years later, I still miss him. He never got to see me play college football. When I married the most wonderful girl in the world his place was vacant. He wasn't there to greet his first grandchildren. When I started a business, he wasn't there to advise me—though I had more counsel from him than I realized at the time, which is a large reason for this book.

———◇◇◇◇———

Seven years after my father's death, I was working for Rev. Jerry Falwell Sr. At a conference at Opryland Hotel in Nashville, we had just settled into our rooms when a call came from home. My twenty-two-year-old brother David was in a car accident and in serious condition. Jerry and I checked out of the hotel, flew to Philadelphia, and drove straight to the Hospital of the University of Pennsylvania.

My kid brother, a wiry go-getter with a knack for making friends, was just home for the summer before his final year at Liberty University. Now he lay comatose next to a row of machines blinking and beeping. His doctors talked with us. Our friend Jerry Falwell prayed with us. Eventually we walked to the hotel across the street where we would stay for the next several days. On June 6, 1986, David Arthur DeMoss joined my father in heaven.

When my father died, I somehow believed that early death would spare the rest of us. Why, I don't know: actuarial tables, conventional wisdom maybe—but certainly not from reading the Bible, which, if anything, underscores life's brevity.

As I begin this third edition of a book on wisdom, I've outlived my father by nearly a decade. My brother's time on earth I've nearly tripled. The math in my head is unavoidable. I have a wife and three children. I have five grandchildren. I've had the thrill and challenges of building a career. I've had adult years and a string of new eras—all things David never lived to experience.

In the early years of the church, the apostle James wrote to Christians in a distant city, "Yet you do not know what your life will be like tomorrow. For you are just a vapor that appears for a little while, and then vanishes away" (James 4:14 NASB).

Just a vapor. What is it about human nature that we so confidently presume on seventy or eighty years of health and life when our Creator doesn't guarantee another breath.

Johnny Williamson was a history teacher and soccer coach at the school my children each attended for thirteen years.

He died on a Thanksgiving Day after an eight-month battle with colon cancer, only thirty-two years old, but his influence on hundreds of young men and women is impossible to express in a book this small. At his memorial service, Johnny's older brother told a standing-room-only crowd the words that Johnny said multiple times in his final days: "I didn't think it would be this soon." He left the world at peace with his Lord but longing for one more semester, one more soccer season.

"A person's days are determined," Job said in his own loss and grief. "You have decreed the number of his months and have set limits he cannot exceed" (Job 14:5 NIV). When my father died, I thought I could never hurt that way again. Then we lost David. Since then, I've shared the great sorrows of other families, and I know to my core what is important. People are. God is. Time is—important, fleeting, priceless.

Winston Churchill's father died at age thirty-nine, and England's most renowned prime minister grew up expecting to die young also. In his first memoir, *My Early Life*, he credits his military exploits, including a dramatic escape atop a moving train, and in general his fearless first decades, to the ticking clock.[1]

My father's death at age fifty-three, in my mind, marked that age in red, a mark all the brighter and more certain for

David's sudden death a handful of years later. I'm never so lost in living that I don't hear the clock or see the calendar, not in a paranoid sense, but with a sense of purpose. As surely as a father's life imprints on a son, a father's early death affects how a son takes on the future . . . and the past, and why he might write a book on wisdom.

I can't recall my father ever wasting even a minute of his life. Not that he was all work—he wasn't—but he made his time count. He played tennis and Monopoly with us. He swam. Conversations, which he loved, were his chances to learn, and think, and impart. He relished professional sporting events; eight months before he died he took my brothers and me to the Super Bowl in Miami. He didn't own a TV; he went to bed at a reasonable hour, even with guests in the living room. ("Turn out the lights when you leave," he'd say as he headed upstairs.) Mornings he rose early because his strong sense of life fully included quiet time with God, and time to think, to plan, to dream.

You can bet my father was on my mind in 2016, eleven days before Christmas, when a phone call put me face-to-face with my mortality. Dr. Roberts' biopsy of a small lump below my jaw wasn't the simple infection he'd suspected, but Diffuse Large B-Cell Lymphoma. I was 54 years old, a year older than Dad was when he dropped dead. After quickly scheduled surgeries to remove the lump and to insert a port in my chest, I started on four months of chemotherapy, which, six years later, appear to have rid my body and bloodstream of all cancer.

To be sure, I didn't "beat" cancer. I was healed of it by the Giver of Life using science and medicine and people and technology. Something besides cancer may permanently close out my days, but cancers—especially blood cancers—are known to return. For now, the chemotherapy infusions, blood draws, and oncology visits bring home to me in yet another way that in our short time on earth we are wise to invest for the greatest return.

When I die, whenever that is, I hope my passing will echo the psalmist's words, "Teach me to number my days, that I may present to You a heart of wisdom" (Psalm 90:12 NASB)—not in the least because my father's life and death continue to show that it's possible.

Preface

Do you see a man wise in his own eyes?
There is more hope for a fool than for
him.

—Proverbs 26:12 (NKJV)

What in the world qualifies a man at age sixty-one to write a book on wisdom, much less a third edition? One answer is that life is a journey and not a destination. On my journey—ahead of some, behind others—as my rear view lengthens so does my regard for sound thinking and good judgment.

In 2007, when this book was first published, I was forty-four years old, a road veteran of decades already, keen to certain practical, essential, and profound applications of wisdom. Another decade and a half further, none of the truths I wrote about have changed but several new ones join them. Fresh illustrations, also, and new statistics, a few more details—and two new chapters—make this third edition worth its own read. Almost weekly, by the way, I still get calls or emails (or letters) from people who have applied a principle and want to say they're better for it. Last month a young businessman told me he rereads *The Little Red Book* once a year.

To the question of what qualifies me to write about wisdom in the first place, my full answer is three-part. First, a friend told me once that wisdom is caught, not taught. From my proximity to certain people and circumstances (more on those as you read), I've had the good fortune to catch wisdom when it counted for everything.

In 1991, I founded a public relations firm called The DeMoss Group (later just DeMoss), my daily door into many of the world's most prominent Christian organizations— helping their leaders know, navigate, and fulfill their missions. For four decades my work looked down the barrel of public opinion, high-stakes media inquiries, prominent personalities, personal crises, and national crises. I joined boardroom deliberations over millions of dollars, thousands of employees, and the futures of large and important causes. Each circumstance, each person, was another case in point of the value of wisdom and the high cost of its absence. Along the way my firm coalesced into a team of talented women and men, ever learning and ever teaching me. Four years since DeMoss closed its doors, I remain in their debt.

I remain in the arena, also, because the "we need help" calls and emails continue, renditions of "I'm on the board of an organization and need advice." Or "Our leader's in hot water and the media are at the door." Or "Protesters plan to disrupt our event." Or "This initiative will shake up a major backlash. How soon can we talk?"

Believe me, I have no lock on wisdom. What I do well is listen, the subject of an entire chapter in this book. In business, *in all of life*, listening is the great unsung skill, the passcode to understanding and discernment, which are the two chief gateways to wisdom.

Second, I'm a student of the greatest wisdom text of all time, the Old Testament book of Proverbs—written and edited by King Solomon, still widely regarded as the sagest man who ever lived. (Another full chapter here urges you to make Proverbs a daily thing.) For more than half of my life I've read a chapter of Proverbs a day—every single day—taking me through all thirty-one chapters close to four hundred times.

Finally, and most important, in the Bible, God makes a wonderful offer: "If any of you lacks wisdom, let him ask of God, who gives to all liberally and without reproach, and it will be given to him" (James 1:5 NKJV).

Solomon was the son of King David, heir to his father's

massive kingdom. One night in a dream God handed Solomon a blank check: "Ask me for anything." In one of the Bible's great stories, Solomon asked for wisdom, "*a discerning heart to know how to govern the people in his charge.*" More than just cash the check, God added riches and honor to the bargain, gifts unequaled in all history.

My frequent prayers for wisdom, for years, have been to handle relationships well, to manage a business and advise clients, to be a good husband and father. Most mornings I begin by asking God for wisdom; most meetings I enter silently asking Him for His insight. God honors His offer, and it comes with no expiration date.

The Little Red Book is my treatise on the wisdom that buttresses my life personally and professionally. The target audience is my three children, and their children, and for every other reader, I'm grateful. Wisdom guides and guards. It calls out to all who listen with counsel that is universal, timeless, and foolproof. May hers be the voice you hear in this book, and not mine.

In closing, the wisdom here is doable. A reader of any age can peruse a chapter of Proverbs a day, listen more and speak less, write letters more, or consistently speak the truth. Wisdom is no respecter of age or beauty, intelligence or education, affluence or sophistication; it calls to everyone, everywhere, always. We need only respond.

PART 1

WISDOM FOR YOUR PROFESSIONAL LIFE

Wisdom is the principal thing;
therefore get wisdom.
—Proverbs 4:7 (KJV)

Chapter 1

STAY UNDER THE UMBRELLA
Finding and Keeping Your Focus in Life

The secret of success is constancy to purpose.
—Benjamin Disraeli, Earl of Beaconsfield

Years ago in Hong Kong, a missionary named John had a genius for getting things done. In a densely populated and difficult city, that sort of thing draws attention, particularly among American businesses salivating over the lucrative Eastern market. One day the ranking executive of a squirt gun manufacturer took John to lunch at a posh city restaurant. In the dining room, the executive slipped $600 to the owner, who led John and his host to a prime corner table.

Napkins had barely hit laps when the manufacturer leaned in. "John," he said, "we're ready to pay you $200,000 a year with a nice office and a car and driver if you come work for us." Perhaps too casually for the executive's pride, John declined the offer (thinking, he said later, he could have saved the guy $600-plus). The exec pressed. "How much are you making now?" he said, and John pressed back. "Eight thousand dollars. But that's not the point. I'm serving God, doing what I'm supposed to do, and I've never been happier."

That night at eleven o'clock John's phone rang. "It's all over Hong Kong you rejected the offer," an agitated voice said. "I would like to know why." The caller refused to take tomorrow for an answer, and forty minutes later, in his pajamas, John was across a coffee table from him. "Everyone at the American Chamber knows," the man said. "I had to hear it for myself."

Years later, recounting the episode to me, John tried to explain why the squirt gun bid and offers like it could never hook him. "I call it 'staying under the umbrella,'" he said. "Step out from under it and you get wet. No amount of money or anything else was going to pull me from my purpose."

John is past eighty now. Last year he buried his wife. Behind him stretches a lifetime of serving people in Europe, Asia, Africa, and dozens of places the names of which most Americans would mispronounce—camps, orphanages, churches, and lives forever changed.

Technically John is retired and unable to globetrot, but the umbrella is still up and overhead. In an age of exploding globalization, he could have had more money, but at the price of much less joy.

What John called staying under the umbrella I call focus—a person's fixed bead on her gifts, purpose, and goals.

How rare is it? Pretty rare. In 2021, a National Longitudinal Survey assessed interviews with ten thousand people in their late teens/early twenties and again in their mid-fifties and early sixties. Their working years averaged twelve jobs a person, four years per employer. Half of the jobs were in the six years between ages eighteen and twenty-four.[1]

Walt Disney told young people to find a job they liked so much they'd do it without compensation, and then to do it so well, people would pay them to continue. Young people today might consider that antiquated. It's priceless.

When résumés came to me (the majority from applicants appearing to want a job, not a career), I looked first at the work history. Common wisdom says jobs in the plural show versatility or ambition. For my money they raise questions. I wanted loyalty, not changeability. Of course bad employers happen, companies downsize, families relocate. We may have to learn what we dislike in order to know what we like. To Walt Disney's point, I'd say the earlier a person has her focus, the longer she has to mature in it and the likelier her long-term success.

———◇◇◇◇◇———

Focus is mission, direction. How many of us have entered an office or workplace ostensibly there to make money or to serve, only to scratch the surface and find no clear purpose?

Mackay Envelope Company was not one of those. Harvey Mackay was twenty-five years old when he founded what recently became the MackayMitchell Envelope Company: five hundred employees cranking out twenty-five million envelopes a day with no end in sight. Mackay preached his practices in seven *New York Times* bestsellers such as *Swim with the Sharks Without Being Eaten Alive.*

I was relatively new in my business when I attended a luncheon in Phoenix with a group of public relations execs, and Harvey Mackay took the podium. I knew next to nothing about him, but he hooked me with a single line. "Our stated mission," he said, "is to be in business forever."

That's it, I thought: *Stick to what you do and do it better than anyone.* No new product lines, no diversifying, just better envelopes and more of 'em. It's too soon to know whether Mackay's business is a "forever" player but he's ninety years old and his envelopes bring in $100 million a year.

Meanwhile, can you name the group that world-renowned management expert Peter Drucker called "by far the most effective organization in the U.S."? Last year its $5.8 billion annual budget served 25 million Americans; its global impact reached 131 countries. The group is the Salvation Army, founded in England in 1865, expanded to the U.S. in 1880, to "preach the gospel of Jesus Christ and meet human needs in His name without discrimination."[2]

How has the Army's confederation of congregations stayed on mission for so long? Commissioner Robert A. Watson is a forty-four-year Army veteran; for four years he was its highest-ranking officer in the U.S. "We operate under the same name and offer our 'customers' the same dual 'product' of salvation and service as we did more than a century ago," he says. By way of context, of the twelve firms on the original Dow Jones Industrials list in 1896, not one is still in today's list of thirty companies.

The Salvation Army has abundant opportunities for new directions, new ways to raise funds, but however great the idea, Commissioner Watson says in *The Most Effective Organization in the U.S.*, "If [it] doesn't advance [salvation and service], we're not interested."[3]

Commitment to mission is nice, you say, but there's also the bottom line. That grows too, Commissioner Watson says, under the mission umbrella: "People trust us to do what we say we're going to do, so they contribute generously." *The Chronicle of Philanthropy* routinely ranks The Salvation Army first among nonprofits, typically raising twice as much support as its fellow blue-chip charities like the American Red Cross and the YMCA.

———◦◦◦◦———

Until four years ago when I became a solo consultant, DeMoss was only my second job out of college, in both cases taking one service to one market: public relations to Christian organizations and causes. My mission stays the same, and I grow and change within it. Mornings I still get up eager to think, to use words and ideas to help inform and shape public opinion.

To draw a line, of course, is to impose a choice. In the way Mackay emphasized envelopes, in the way the Salvation Army served "the least of these" in Jesus' name, the line we drew at DeMoss helped protect us from wrong choices, however lucrative or well-intentioned. We were in PR, not fundraising, media time sales, video production, or tele-marketing. Those skills we left to companies with other focuses or no focus.

One time we had a chance at an enticing summerlong contract to promote a major sports drink. The manufacturer sought us out, the work seemed to be ours for the taking, and the project looked fun, with interesting new markets and contacts. We debated taking it, but only briefly because sports drinks had nothing to do with our mission.

If you're overdue to know your mission, the common advice is to start with your interests. What makes your heart leap? What moves you or angers you? When you lose all sense of time, what are you doing? If you don't know, ask people who know you. Take the time to look at yourself and to work out a brief personal mission statement (the briefer the statement, the harder the work). Then begin a day at a time, a decision at a time, to deflect the good and pursue the great.

Whether you're called to help make twenty-five million envelopes a day, serve 171 million meals a year, raise children, provide a service, build a company, or plant a garden, when you know your focus, pursue the freedom of discipline.

Or in the words of the missionary who turned down millions: find your umbrella and stay under it.

Chapter 2

TACKLE SOMETHING SO DIFFICULT YOU'LL NEVER WANT TO DO IT AGAIN
Exit Your Comfort Zone

I don't want to fall off the lowest
rung on the ladder.
—Sting

On a Monday in early June at 7:45 A.M., a college man named Dan Pinkney pulled up to a housing subdivision and gestured to me in the back seat. "There's your first house," he said. "Meet you back here at nine tonight."

I was sixteen, and whatever a salesperson is I wasn't. I climbed out of the car and reached back in for my small case of books. Then I turned and placed one foot in front of the other until my body stood before an aluminum-screened front door. The summer between my junior and senior years of high school, for thirteen hours a workday, I would be pounding the pavement in small-town Pennsylvania. Home was two hours down the interstate but a universe away.

The Southwestern Company of Nashville, Tennessee, did then what it does today: train college students for door-to-door book sales and fan them into neighborhoods across the country. My friend and sales manager, Dan, was a veteran of six Southwestern summers, an extroverted purveyor of books. A few weeks before I had been a contented introvert, unpressured to earn money for college or anything else. But my father knew sales, he knew life, and he knew me. And here I was, leaving Dan's car to lug books on sidewalks and knock on strangers' doors.

I had immersed myself in the Southwestern system during a week of intense training days that were part pep rally, part classroom training, a big part memorization and mock sales presentations. My division sold a topical Bible, a set of six thin children's books, and a medical encyclopedia, the irresistible logic being that a home with kids or grandkids needed a medical encyclopedia and more children's reading. And what household couldn't use a topical Bible?

Most Southwestern trainees were there for the money. The stars might earn a thousand dollars or more per week. My family was financially comfortable; my education was covered. Most of my peers would take it easy that summer or work light jobs in the final break as rising high school seniors. The other mental minefield for me was the DeMoss family vacation that summer on the Caribbean island of St. Croix—our final getaway with my father, though we couldn't know it then. While my six siblings took in beaches and ocean breezes, I would haul hardbound books up hot, humid neighborhood sidewalks and back down again. Which sidewalks? Territory assignments came at the end of training and not a minute before.

Even Dan couldn't say where we'd spend our summer. Florida? I hoped for somewhere fun. Chicago? Out West? Late on a Saturday night we got our orders for Mechanicsburg, Pennsylvania. In a few hours my team was loaded into Dan's car with a map, sales cases, and a few dollars—no salary, no expense advance, no lead on that night's room and board. On Sunday afternoon we reached Mechanicsburg and pulled up at a gas station telephone booth. (Remember those?) Someone found a phone book and began calling area churches for places to stay. One had a retired couple with two upstairs bedrooms, which we took sight unseen, landing us among the fortunate few. Some reps would stay in temporary quarters for weeks. But that part was incidental. Come Monday morning, we would all be out selling.

That first Sunday night we unpacked in our rooms, then gathered with Dan, who unfolded a local map, pulled out a yellow highlighter, and divided the neighborhoods into sales territories. Before we turned in, one last time a veteran and three know-nothings rehearsed their presentations.

I was a seventy-five-hour man now, up at six o'clock, by eight o'clock greeting my first prospects; by 9:00 P.M. I was wrapping final sales. Monday through Friday—Saturdays, eight to six—the goal was to knock on eighty doors a day and make thirty sales presentations. On Southwestern's 42 percent commission, one Bible sale a day would net out at $27, about $2 per hour.

In the beginning, the thirteen-hour days dragged to infinity and beyond. Between houses, my feet moved glacially. Lunch was slow, and in the standstill afternoons, I would check to make sure my watch was working. I was no salesman. I was lonely and intimidated. A call to my comfort zone would have been long-distance. The worst part wasn't the endless hours and strange surroundings—the worst part was the rejection. On good days the doors closed in our faces. Most days they slammed, though eventually I came to appreciate the slammers for not wasting my time.

To this day my mother remembers her anguish during my weekly calls. Several times Dad refused to put her on the phone because she was in the background saying, "Art, please let him come home if he wants to. Tell him he doesn't have to stay out there."

Saturday nights my colleagues and I joined fifty or so other Southwestern student salespeople at a local college for meetings like the training-week pep rallies, now featuring sales reports, success stories, selling tips, and a speaker's long-winded challenge to up our numbers. At first the Saturday nights brought familiar faces. Then those faces began to disappear as my fellow booksellers dumped the long hours and unknown income for forty-hour workweeks with guaranteed pay back home. (Fifty-five percent of the first-year student sellers still throw in the towel in their first weeks.)

Inside me something altogether different was happening. For one thing, I had a few sales under my belt. For another, and to my surprise, the sight of *college* students cashing in didn't discourage me. It hardened my resolve to stick it out and even make some serious money.

Forty-some-odd years later, I can still recall the Great Shift. Where once I checked my watch for Dan's arrival, I estimated hours left against doors and potential presentations. Where I had lingered over lunch, now I skipped it. When a sympathetic family would invite me to stay for dinner, I'd weigh a helping of casserole against the loss in sales time and a spot in the Saturday night rankings and politely decline. Late each day as darkness fell, my eyes scanned for one more house, one more prospect, one more sale.

Before the clock ran down that summer I was determined to sell $1,000 worth of books in a single week. In the final push I squeaked over the top with a Bible I sold to myself. Yessir, I could sell. In a handful of months, I learned to love hard work, to turn undaunted from a door in my face,

14

to budget my time, to speak so that people would listen. I learned that customers buy the person selling rather than the product. While my friends cruised suburban Philly in their parents' cars, that first summer as a licensed driver I learned to get my foot in the door. Mornings I took cold showers to wake up and to resist lingering under the steamy water (though that character-builder ended with the summer).

A dozen years later when I founded a public relations firm in a new niche, I did it with no agency experience, not even an internship. But by then three months of cold calls in Mechanicsburg, Pennsylvania, had aged into mental rocket fuel. To this day, I have never had a harder job or better training for everything that came after.

The record should show that during my last year of high school, I turned down a chance to sell the next summer. Dan asked me to recruit my own team, adding student commissions to my personal sales income. Dan was a good salesman, but the truth is that I feared it. It was that tough, and I passed.

Southwestern still trains fifteen hundred student salespersons by the summer, their twelve-week grosses ranging from $6,500 for newbies to nearly $30,000 for third-years and $70,000 for five-timers. Its alumni roster includes governors and senators, corporate founders, CEOs, presidents, and every kind of entrepreneur. Too bad today's security worries, gated communities, and similar "advancements" discourage door-to-door sales. The herculean quest to persevere in work

I initially hated forever changed how I would take on life's challenges.

All that said, that summer was about my father, not me. I had no sense that a face-off against shyness could ultimately save me from myself. All I had was my father's direction. He knew what I needed. He loved me enough not to spare me the tough route.

Because of him I learned that business begins where my knuckle meets the door. I learned that if I can't do it without fear then do it afraid; reward rides with risk. Sales is person-to-person. On the far side of anxiety is growth, which for other people may involve a return to school, extended missions, an overdue conversation—or pursuing public office, running a marathon, or writing a book. In my late twenties it had me launching a public relations firm.

The ache of missing my father only intensified when the summer ended, and he left us for good. Until then the miles between us were hard on him, hard on me, hard on my mother, and we stuck it out. And the last thing my father ever asked of me was a crash course in what every father wants most for his son: it helped me become a man.

Chapter 3

THE AMAZING POWER OF UNDERSTATEMENT
Under-Promise, Over-Deliver

Less is more.
—Robert Browning, "Andrea del Sarto"

From the front offices of the *Washington Post*, we entered a richly paneled boardroom where editors, reporters, columnists, and executives outnumbered our small group five or six to one. We took our seats, and while waiters in tuxedos served lunch, I pondered what careers had been derailed or destroyed in the kind of interrogation we'd come for.

The year was 1997. Seven years earlier a college football coach named Bill McCartney had founded a ministry-turned-movement called Promise Keepers. Across the U.S. a succession of conferences had filled stadiums, touching a national nerve leading now to "Stand in the Gap—A Sacred Assembly of Men" on the National Mall in Washington, D.C. The groundswell had pushed Coach McCartney to the front lines of national and international media, most often to promote the phenomena, today to explain Stand in the Gap.

Coach was no stranger to the press. A few years before he'd led the University of Colorado to a national championship. This was no competition, however, not for us, though the road to the National Mall is paved with the ambitions of groups eager to flex their political muscle. Our power would show in the turnout: the larger the crowd, the stronger the statement.

For most gatherings on the National Mall the trick was to get a crowd count in the absence of turnstiles, fixed seating, or gate receipts. Until Stand in the Gap, to start the momentum, a typical host organization would predict a record-breaking attendance. Later at the actual event, the U.S. Park Police would release an official crowd estimate. Invariably that estimate would undercut the host's predictions, and the host would accuse the park police of bias.

That day in the *Post* boardroom, the crowd estimate was almost first in line. "So, Coach, how many people are you expecting?"

As Promise Keepers' official spokesperson, I spoke up: "We won't project a number now," I said, preempting Coach's natural enthusiasm. "We won't estimate a number that day, and we won't debate your number the next day." A room of journalists used to spin and sparring with their newsmaker guests looked as if we'd rolled over and played dead. "We expect a lot of men," I said hopefully, "but have no idea how many." The logic was obvious, but our media heavyweights seemed unaccustomed to modesty.

As for third-party crowd estimates, earlier that year the National Park Service had ended them. Too many public spats with groups insisting on bigger numbers. That change suited us. Where most groups filled the mall to show dominance, Promise Keepers hoped to show humility. "No political speeches that day," we told the Post. "Nothing about legislation. No local or national dignitaries on the platform, elected or unelected. No signed petitions. No slogans."

The optic of a sea of men committed to What Matters would say all we had to say, though for some people it was a tough stopping point. Weeks earlier, one of Coach's staff members found a local aerial photography company able to download photos instantly for precise crowd figures, and we discouraged it, even for internal records. "If the crowd is big, we won't *need* an official number," I said. "If it's small, we won't *want* a number."

At last the Saturday in October came, and so did the men. From just after midnight until the official start at ten o'clock that morning, miles of buses streamed in and unloaded. We issued media credentials to eleven hundred reporters and camera people. C-SPAN aired the full eight hours live to ninety million homes. From the capitol steps to the Washington Monument, from across America and dozens of nations besides, men filled the gap, spilling into side streets and neighborhoods. Some media organizations estimated up to a million participants, dubbing Stand in the Gap one of the largest gatherings ever held in the nation's capital.

And we held our tongue, giving the journalists nothing to challenge, nothing to attack, no means to label the day anything but what it was. The pictures said what no boast could.

"Under-promise, over-deliver," we'd say at DeMoss, and so we advised our clients. A quarter century later, Stand in the Gap remains a testament both to restraint and to focus. We stayed under the umbrella. We knew our purpose and kept to it. We earned the media's respect, and it came out in the coverage.

I have yet to see a public program fail for avoiding puff. I also have a bulging clip file of bold predictions snatching defeat from the jaws of victory. A leader or spokesperson publicly predicts sixty thousand attendees, twenty thousand show up, and reputations take a hit. Shame on the hosts. Twenty thousand people is small relative only to the pre-event braggadocio, so why do it? Life has enough shortfalls without creating our own.

A few years after Promise Keepers' day in D.C., another

religious group staged an event on the National Mall. This group poured two years into planning. It had strong local support and a history of large crowds worldwide. Its spokesperson boldly predicted a hundred thousand attendees, and *The Washington Post* duly reported it. On opening night ten thousand people showed up—no small feat in that October night's low temps and heavy rains. But weather didn't dampen the group's reputation. They did it to themselves, needing somehow to feel big before the fact.

———◇◇◇◇◇———

Around that time a global Christian leader announced a new nonprofit in Africa to "save a million orphans from the AIDS epidemic" mobilizing people and resources to house thousands of children. The leader promised to build an industrial park and an entire educational system on thousands of acres. The African nation's leaders watched, wondering, perhaps, if it was too good to be true.

And it was. Not a spade of ground was broken when the same international Christian leader went back to the microphone to term the project "the largest humanitarian religious movement in the history of the world from the U.S. to Africa." Why the big talk? I don't know. I know that four months later he resigned from the organization and left the continent, leaving a new president and a bewildered staff to bear the burden of his public pledge. "I'll put it down as one of the disappointments of my career," he said later.

In that developing nation, a project a fraction of the announced size and scope would have made history. The speaker had an impressive record of large accomplishments and nothing to prove. Thousands of Christians heeded his call, leaving their homes to plant hundreds of thousands of vegetable gardens, enabling impoverished families to grow their own food. The project exceeded expectations and was lifting a nation. Why the hype? The overblown declaration hit a wall and morale fell into a heap.

———◦◦◇◦◦———

The field of PR, *my field*, gets slapped with labels like *spin*, *puff*, or *hype*, and too often for good reason. Once I came across Hype Public Relations, claiming "unparalleled success in establishing credibility and brand awareness" for its clients. What self-respecting company would hand its reputation to a firm of that name? Hype means deceit. Hyperbole means "greatly overstates or exaggerates"—hardly a calling card for "establishing credibility" and long-term trust.

Our firm was anti-hype, to our fiscal harm when potential clients wanted hard sell from us on soft evidence. But unless the project or person merited the attention, we couldn't in good conscience take their money.

Once at an introductory meeting with a fairly new client, we mentioned that philosophy, and he stopped us to let the words sink in. He said, "You may change our view of public relations," and I like to think we did.

From years of work with all kinds of people in the public eye, I can attest that great leaders are first of all great servants, happy to understate, happy to tamp down the rhetoric and let the work speak for them.

I define understatement as judicious restraint, the kind Jesus referred to when He said, "Blessed are the meek" (Matthew 5:5)—calling us to the opposite of weakness. In a world of hype, that kind of understatement is power.

Chapter 4

WORK LESS, THINK MORE
Better Still, Work on Thinking

*Thinking is the hardest work there is, which is
probably the reason why so few engage in it.*
—Henry Ford

Companies paid $450,000 and up for Joey Reiman's ideas, some of them taking him less than a month to conceive. CEO Jim Adamson of the Advantica Restaurant Group would broadcast to anyone that he happily paid Joey Reiman a million dollars "just to think!" Those were the days when Joey headed BrightHouse, "the world's first ideation corporation" (later acquired by the behemoth Boston Consulting Group). Joey's autobiography, aptly titled *Thinking for a Living*,[1] toured readers through both sides of his brain. One of my associates gave me the book, and I was better for the trip.

One chapter in, I ordered copies for my entire staff and made it required reading. Then I scheduled an off-site session to explore how we could all upgrade our thinking, individually, and as a firm. The morning of the session, I told my children that DeMoss was closed for the day to think about *thinking* and I got three puzzled looks. Most grownups, sadly, would have reacted the same way.

In the book, Joey invites readers to write to him, and I did that too. I told him he'd turned my firm into a one-author book club, and I invited him to meet and speak to his new fans at a "thinking lunch."

Joey's office called with his yes to our lunch meeting, and we paid him around $1,500. The chance to tap his mind was great, but the wonder of that time together was his sheer enthusiasm for thinking, my mantra since day one. He invited any of us to drop by the BrightHouse headquarters in Atlanta, but with a caveat. "You won't find people hustling and bustling about," he said. "They'll be in their offices with their feet propped on their desks, *thinking*," and he mentioned again his half-million-dollar fees.

So Mr. Reiman could entertain and motivate, but hundreds of thousands of dollars for a month of work? *Marketing sizzle*, I thought, and dismissed it until five years later over lunch with an executive at a major corporation in the Southeast. He told me they were well into a month of paid thinking from BrightHouse.

"I need to ask you something," I said.

"It's true," he said without waiting for my question.

"The fee?"

"Half a million," he said. And he said it in a "bargain-at-twice-the-price" tone.

There's a conversation to be had about thinking and doing. The corporate world—no, the *world*—wants to see furious *doing*: designing, scheduling, writing, building, producing, implementing . . . which is fine when it comes with thinking, but too often it doesn't.

Public relations has a lot of doing that DeMoss didn't do. First and fundamentally our clients needed strong thinking. News releases, press conferences, and interviews, for us to use them, had to serve a purpose. We were in business to shape public opinion, not to shuffle papers and send emails. But that approach was uncommon.

Why think hard and then think harder? Because, according to world-class thinker Albert Einstein, "We cannot solve our problems with the same level of thinking that created them."[2]

And where are the thinkers today? Blocked, I think, behind two largely cultural obstacles. The first is the time and quiet to think clearly and well amid smartphones, iPads, laptops, books, magazines, television, radio, meetings, email, video games, Meta (Facebook), YouTube, Twitter, Instagram, TikTok, Snapchat, and Pinterest. Americans last year, per person, averaged 144 minutes (two hours-plus) a day on social media, for a minimum fourteen waking hours a week when thinking was a lost cause.[3] Add to that three hours gone to TV and five-plus hours spent on email.

Thinking is on life support. *Thinking*. Not one more item on a multitasker's list. Not a discussion point, but a chief requisite to live and move and be. And we've lost touch with it. Reiman said when people hear what he does for a living they inevitably ask, "What does a thinker think about?" to which he says, "Everything."

"Everything" is the right answer, but in the twenty-first century to think on even a few things has to be intentional. A person has to want to function for an hour or two a day beyond the reach of a screen. Or to exercise without SportsCenter or a podcast blaring. In all that listening, what are we losing? I'll say this, any day you choose to both exercise and think, you'd be solving problems and spawning ideas at least thirty minutes a day more than the guy on the next treadmill or the woman passing you on the path.

Warren Buffett, the world's greatest investor, heads Berkshire Hathaway, a $730 billion investment firm of 372,000 employees. His personal worth exceeds $100 billion (after giving $50 billion to charity). Warren Buffett also is a walking testament to thinking vs. doing. Or having. So if you're picturing him in a Wall Street office tower, picture again. Because he lives in Omaha, Nebraska, the town he was born in and never left.

"You can think here," Mr. Buffett says. "You can think better about the market. You don't hear so many stories, and you can just sit and look at the stock on the desk in front of you. You can think about a lot of things."[4] This from a man whose company stock trades above $500,000 per share, in 2021 topping revenues of $276 billion.

I can't say it directly enough: Be like Warren Buffett. Order your life to think more. If you can't move to the Midwest, make dates with solitude. One or two noon hours a week, do lunch alone. I did four or five days a week, not to be unsocial, and not because I'm a quiet guy, but to read and think, or write and think, or plan and think.

Back in 2007 as I was writing this book's first edition, a business title at a Barnes & Noble leapt into my hands: *Never Eat Alone, and Other Secrets to Success, One Relationship at a Time*. The author's premise is that a rising business star uses every minute of every workday to network, schmooze, trade business cards, connect, and/or follow up.

Not me. Profit built only on doing is as fragile as it is shortsighted. Human contact is good. I'm pro-relationship. But when thinking is a priority, then a lunch alone—a chance in a busy day to pause for perspective—is a terrible thing to waste.

A second obstacle to good thinking is that too few people and organizations value or demand it. Most people are busy doing what they've always done, as if motion alone justifies a paycheck. I submit that when a doer also is an intentional thinker, or backed by one, the motion gains new traction.

It might also gain new uses. "Great thinkers think

inductively," Joey Reinman says. "They create the solution and seek out the problems the solution might solve; most companies think *deductively*, that is, defining a problem and then investigating different solutions."[5]

Time magazine once put Dallas pastor T. D. Jakes on its cover over the words "America's Best Preacher."[6] Having heard him many times on television, in person—and "off script"—I endorse that label. April and I had the good fortune to host a dinner for him in our home one evening, followed by an intimate conversation with our forty guests. That night he gave us a glimpse of his mental cogs and gears. "I'm always thinking," he said. "My preaching is just the verbalization of what I'm processing. *I'm really a better thinker than I am a preacher.*"

My firm's early technical knowhow was average at best. After all, I'd never taken a college course on the subject, never even interned at a PR firm. But our emphasis on thinking, I came to believe, more than compensated for our PR learning curve even as it distinguished us from much of our competition.

To wrap up this train of thinking, the lopsided ratio of headwork to hand work has excellent precedents. In 1501, when the Arte della Lana commissioned Michelangelo to sculpt a statue of David, Michelangelo was given the same block of marble that Agostino di Duccio had unsuccessfully tried to sculpt forty years earlier. As the story goes, every day for three months the twenty-six-year-old Michelangelo stared at the marble block, leaving at the end of a workday and returning the next morning to stare again, day after day, to the puzzlement of onlookers.

"What are you doing?" someone finally asked him.

"Working," the master sculptor said.

Think about it.

Chapter 5

TECHNOLOGY ISN'T EVERYTHING
Use It Wisely

Technology . . . the knack of so arranging the
world that we don't have to experience it.
—Max Frisch

One day at the DeMoss homestead our high-speed internet lost its zip and we had the good fortune to welcome a live service technician. Where the street cable met our house, he set up a mystical box. "Ah," he said after a while, "no wonder. Not enough juice in the line." With a few adjustments in another black box, he pronounced us back in business, packed up his meter box, and drove away.

Back in our home, the internet still moved like a three-year-old getting up early, which is to say not at all. The next morning I dialed, er, punched in the cable company telephone number—an office a mere two miles away—to schedule a quick and easy return visit.

Welcome to Cable Communications. For quality assurance

31

purposes, your call may be monitored. Please enter your ten-digit phone number.

So far, so good. I knew my phone number.

To make a payment on your account, or for account balance information, press 1.

To order new service or to add additional service, press 2.

If you are experiencing technical difficulties with any of our products, press 3.

For billing questions, press 4.

To disconnect or remove service, press 5.

I paused, considering my options.

If you'd like to hear this menu again, press 9.

No number matched my situation, so I pressed 9, hoping for the nice fellow from the night before. For a second time the recording ran through my five options, and I pressed 3.

If you would like to confirm a previously scheduled appointment, press 1.

No . . . nothing about a previously scheduled appointment. I needed to *discuss* an appointment from the previous evening.

To reset your converter box, press 2.

No converter box at our house.

For cable TV support, press 3. For high-speed internet support, press 4.

Every new press of a number took me further afield. The positive-sounding female voice urged me to go to a website, but wasn't internet reception my presenting problem? The voice listed more options touching on everything but the reason for my call.

Then came the longed-for words:

To speak with a customer service representative, please press 0.

I pressed 0 and no human materialized. By now I was late for the office, and I gave up.

On the way to the garage, when I groused to April about our quagmire, she offered to pick up where I left off. "No," I said. "I'll drop by their office and do it in person."

"Don't waste your time," she said, "I've tried that. It's not a real office. They just refer you to their toll-free number or website."

And so it goes in homes across the nation in our near-total dependency on mostly service-free technology. It's great when it works, and when it doesn't we're talking (or screaming) to ourselves. To add to the frustration, less that ten percent of customers, says Gartner Research, reported resolving their issues via self-service without phone assistance.[1]

But reverting to a telephone menu for technical help is like leaving a bad car for a busted bicycle. *Can* a company calm customer rage over technology with more technology? Another study (frustration begets studies) shows thirty-seven percent of callers to automated systems will press 0 immediately to speak with a human. One blogger has an online "cheat sheet" for reaching live operators at top companies.[2]

Several pastors whom I sometimes call—at large churches, to be fair—are as tied up in call-routing technology as the most "progressive" corporations. Their systems work as long as my need fits snugly into one of half a dozen options. In those cases a black box somewhere in the building can speed me to another black box. But for all the miracles of ones and zeros, no box detects the urgency in my voice. No electronic impulse pokes its head down the hall to tell me the pastor's assistant is at the copier—or about to end the call she's on now. No sensor knows the associate and pastor are ready for my call. And while we all wait to talk, while we're all on the line and sitting on go, the human connection lags for hours and sometimes days.

A caller to DeMoss was sent to voicemail for two reasons and two reasons only: 1) if the call came at night, or 2) if the caller *requested* voicemail. For twenty-eight years, between 8:30 A.M. and 6:00 P.M., callers to DeMoss spoke with an informed human being. Sherry or Lisa or Erin knew where to find anyone. They knew what calls were expected. They knew when any of us left the office and when our flights were due to land. In the nine or ten hours of a standard work-day, no call to DeMoss fell into the digital abyss. When I was unavailable, people needing me could talk to a competent colleague—outperforming even the most sophisticated voicemail system. Until we closed our doors for good in 2019, this dinosaur of a policy reigned.

———◇◇◇◇———

Now to email—one giant step for mankind, one great leap backward for the human arts of thinking, conversing, and personal exchange. In 2002, the industrialized world (and beyond) emailed and received 400,000 terabytes of information—the entire Library of Congress *forty thousand* times over (the figure is now beyond tracking, I believe). To that, factor in how an incoming email rips a recipient from his project, his focus on a phone conversation, or any one of a list of activities.

Think about it. Please. When letters arrived from the U.S. Postal Service, did you stop everything and open them to immediately reply? Even now, when an overnight FedEx appears on your desk, do you unpack it right then? Where is it written that an electronic message owns the moment? Seldom did I walk our office hallway without someone asking me if I'd read an email sent moments before. I usually said no.

Most men and women of the workforce go to work fully intending to turn out a day's work, only to wrap up eight or nine hours later with nothing but answered email to their credit. It's possible, I now believe, to spend an entire career (and life, maybe) like Pavlov's dogs, answering email and hitting send, answering email and hitting send, answering email and hitting send, answering email and hitting send.

For hours a day I work where the computer on my desk

can't find me—at a table or on a sofa. It takes discipline. It's hard to ignore bells and dings. But it's my agenda or someone else's. I consciously choose to pursue what my generation bypasses and a new generation may never learn, namely the time to think and read and discuss and write.

Warren Buffett spends most of his days with no computer nearby. He's on the phone then, you say, talking to people who are on computers. Nope. A *Wall Street Journal* reporter who spent a day on the job with Buffett said the world's richest man received a whopping thirteen phone calls that day, including one wrong number.

I am not anti-technology. As blogs became a thing, our firm paid an industry expert $10,000 for a day-long course on their effective use. Even as a boutique firm we led in technology—updating and replacing our capacities and capabilities earlier and more often than any group we knew of. Our phone system, however, always the latest and greatest by any standard, had to adapt to our human emphasis and not the other way around. With every digital advance, our culture had to enable our workers to think, speak, plan, and write—pursuits that, done well, require time unplugged.

The issue never, never was technology vs. no technology. The issue was to conform technology to my life and not the other way around. You've heard the saying "We make the technology and then it makes us." Not if I can help it. I decide when I read an email and when I answer it. My timely response may or may not match the speed of instant messaging, and so what?

If this is sounding like a manifesto, it is. When technology ceases to be an aid, I cease to use it. I own an iPhone not to read email on the walk to the restroom but to make prudent use of downtime in a taxicab or an airport lounge. (FYI, no beep, tone, or vibration alerts me to your email. I'll read it when I check my inbox.)

Americans are drowning in information that no one asks for. In 2018 90 percent of the world's data had materialized in the previous two years. Five years ago the average person processed seventy-four gigabytes of information a day, more than double the intake eight years before. Seventy-four gigabytes is like watching sixteen movies.

"The art of being wise," William James, the nineteenth century philosopher, said, "is the art of knowing what to overlook."[3] Tell that to the California woman in the news for 300,000 text messages in one month (that's 6.9 a minute, twenty-four hours a day). Extreme? Sure, but look at the average habits. A 2022 study from Pew Internet and American Life says teens exchange a hundred-plus texts a day for thirty-two hundred a month.[4] With apologies to William James, we're not overlooking, we're overtaken.

If you're among the nearly one hundred and ten million people following Katy Perry on Twitter, you're treated to nuggets like this: "Sorry kids, chickens don't have fingers." Or this: "Fr tho what makes you lose sleep? For me it's drinking coffee after 6pm. Leave ur insomniac excuses in the comments." Or "teenagers will save us all." On Elon Musk's $44 billion platform, the singer speaks to twice as many people as the prime minister of India, the most populous democracy in the world.

Millions on millions of adults on Twitter follow millions on millions of other adults for newsy updates on where someone ate lunch, temperatures in Portland, a plane still sitting on the tarmac, and how many emails piled up through a busy day of meetings. Any wonder that 44 percent of Twitter accounts have never sent a tweet?

One celebrity musician with millions of followers left Twitter in 2010 with this thoughtful send-off: "It occurred to me that since the invocation of Twitter, nobody who has participated in it has created any lasting art. And yes! Yours truly is included in that roundup as well.

"Those who remain offline will make better work than those online," the star went on. "Why? Because great ideas have to gather. They have to pass the test of withstanding thirteen different moods, four different months, and sixty different edits. Anything less is day trading. You can either get a bunch of mentions now, or change someone's life next year."[5]

I think of the musings of the late Dutch Catholic priest Henri Nouwen: "Why do we human beings learn so much, so soon, about technology," he wrote, "and so little, so late, about loving one another?"[6]

Years ago, pre–social media—when it was hard enough to practice civility—I resolved to be present to the people I'm with. As social media moved in, I resolved to live unenslaved to its digital distractions. Each decision pushed me against the current. Of ten people at a boardroom table, six or seven will also be in cyberspace, thumbs flying. At dinners out, a phone will sound. In an intense conversation, a text chimes. And while technology saps our workdays, our community lives, our friendships, our solitude, our minds, and our thinking, I remind myself that life comes with no rewind.

In 2009 at the University of Pennsylvania, the commencement speaker told graduates that to live is to unplug. "You're actually going to have to turn off your phone and discover all that is human around us," he challenged the future leaders. "Nothing beats holding the hand of your grandchild as he walks his first steps."[7]

That good advice sounds standard until you know that the speaker was Eric Schmidt, then chair of Google. The search engine was only ten years old then; I wonder what the retired king of instant information would have to say to graduating seniors now.

Chapter 6

Buy Some Stamps
Reclaiming the Lost Art of Letter Writing

To send a letter is a good way to move somewhere
without moving anything but your heart.
—Phyllis Theroux

Check your mailbox. The real one, for letters with stamps and postage marks. If you're a typical American, for every hundred pieces of mail you find there, you'll have one personal letter. Even then not a letter per se. Most likely it'll be a greeting card, an announcement, or an invitation.

For the past decade, with each passing year Americans have written and mailed a billion fewer letters. As I write, first-class mail volume is at a fifty-year low. The obvious blame goes to email, but the regrettable decline of pen on paper began not with digits and bytes but with the drop in prices for long-distance phone calls. Our noblest habits fall to convenience. Goodbye thoughtful, lasting, handwritten (or even typed) words on paper. I mourn your passing.

I mourn it, and I resist it. One Saturday recently I hand-wrote and mailed thirteen letters. Why? Because it matters. Near Christmas one year I sent handwritten notes to thirty-four people I'd worked with through the year. Email and cell phones have their places, but for human expression to outlast electronic impulses, I invest the time and money to write and send real mail.

Incidentally, since the first release of this book, it's this chapter that consistently draws the most response. I've received hundreds and hundreds of *letters*—the writers ranging from a sixteen-year-old student to a ninety-one-year-old widow. Not only do I save the letters, I answer every single one on stationery that I put in an envelope with a stamp and slot into a mailbox. Many of my correspondents write to say they are taking up letter writing or resuming it. One woman proudly informed me she now mails out five handwritten notes a day.

In a treasure of a *New York Times* piece, James Fallows, a national correspondent for the *Atlantic Monthly*, mourns the nearly extinct pleasure of a letter that someone has taken the time to write, fold, seal, and mail. "To leaf through a box of old paper correspondence is to know what has been lost in the shift," Fallows writes. "The pretty stamps, the varying look and feel of handwritten and typed correspondence, the tangible object that was once in the sender's hands."[1]

Tangible, there's a word. Personal letters are tangible

history writ small—loves, milestones, the daily news of nations, soldiers, friends, scientists, statesmen, sweethearts . . . and other people we know and love. The collected letters of historymakers like Ronald Reagan or George Bush break them into the sums of their relationships, their days, their observations, thoughts, personalities, and reactions. A letter kept is a door into times when thoughts were fresh and worth shaping, when people and words deserved our effort.

A book called *Letters of the Century* does that for me, like a time machine amplifying voices from handwritten lines behind the headlines. As a father and grandfather, especially after the COVID-19 pandemic, I'm moved as if it were today by a mother's letter from 1955.

In 1948, polio epidemics began sweeping through the U.S., crippling and killing tens of thousands of young children every year. Finally, in 1955, a physician/researcher named Jonas Salk announced that he had found a successful vaccine for the disease. The next day an expectant mother wrote to him with "the blessings of a million mothers to whom your discovery means freedom from a most tragic fear."

I feel her words even as I write them. "The difference between knowing that Americans were grateful to Jonas Salk and reading this letter to him is like the difference between knowing the words to a song and hearing it sung," the book's editors wrote. "Letters give history a voice."[2]

A "Mail Moment" from a Postal Service survey ended with a bittersweet note that "two-thirds of all consumers do not expect to receive personal mail, but when they do, it makes their day." That hope, the survey said, keeps people coming back. Fifty-five percent of Americans look forward to the possibilities in each day's mail, for goodness' sake.[3] Why do we disappoint them?

On June 19, 1979, my father sat down and wrote to me in Mechanicsburg, Pennsylvania, where I was spending the summer selling books. Seventy-four days later he would be gone, dead of a heart attack. But that June day he was thinking of me, writing on the beautiful letterhead of the company he built.

Dear Mark:

It was good chatting with you last night, and I'm glad to see how enthused you are about what you will be doing this summer.

Again, I am confident this will prove to be a great and wonderfully worthwhile experience, regardless of how little or much money you earn. As you indicated, the discipline itself will be excellent and I am sure the experience will prove to be invaluable in whatever you decide to do with your life.

We really miss you already! Selfishly, we wish

you were here with us. But I know this is going to be in your best interest. I am praying especially for these first few days during this time of getting acclimated, after which I feel sure the whole thing will become much easier.

With much love,
Dad

P.S. I want you to know—I'm very proud of you!

Here was my mail moment. The letter is typed; the P.S. is in Dad's hand. Now it's in my hand, this last-ever piece of him specifically for me, one hundred sixty words of love and encouragement with his priceless perspective on money, his empathy, his belief in me brimming with pride.

Not long after I married, my sister worked in the U.S. Senate for Jesse Helms of North Carolina. When she told him about the birth of our first child, he took the time to write to us:

Dear Mark and April:

Dorothy and I have been so excited about the arrival of Georgia Ann, and want to meet that young lady at the first opportunity. Since she'll be three months old next week, I wonder how much she weighs now.

While I know there's no shortage of Bibles and New Testaments in your home, perhaps you'll want to put the enclosure in a drawer so, some years hence, Georgia Ann will know that there was an old Senator who loved her even before he met her.

I hope you three are doing well, and we send our affectionate best wishes to you.

God bless you always.

Sincerely,
Jesse

Eighteen months later, our mailbox held another envelope from the U.S. Senate:

Dear Mark and April—and Georgia!

There was a real angel gracing your lovely Christmas card this year—but I cannot believe Georgia has already become a captivating young lady. She is gorgeous.

Right after the election, I had to come right back here to participate in the Ethics Committee hearings—which just seem to go on and on, and on and on. I do so much want to be home with the children and grandchildren, instead of being here.

You have brightened my day, and I am so deeply grateful.

Several times during past years, I have sent special friends the text of a Christmas prayer delivered in the Senate more than 50 years ago by Dr. Peter Marshall. I have been pleasantly surprised that many friends have asked me to do that again this year.

Thank you for your friendship, and best wishes for a joyful and meaningful Holy season—and a Happy New Year!

Sincerely,
Jesse

We lived in Virginia at the time, outside of Senator Helms' state and constituency. How many letters he wrote during his thirty-year Senate career, I can't know. On the theory that people tend to behave consistently, more than a few folks must have valued greetings, handwritten, from this man whom they admired. Our sweet Georgia was a few years old when April and I took her to Washington, D.C., and to Sen. Helms' office. He was as gracious in person as he was on paper.

———◦◦◦◦◦———

Where letter writing is practiced, some will leave indelible prints on hearts and souls. That's a big part of the magic. Golf great Phil Mickelson, in a book titled *One Magical Sunday*, tells about his 2004 Masters win, his first "major." He'd won twenty-three PGA tournaments, but given his aggressive style of play, critics said he'd never add a major to his resume.

The day of his first Masters victory, reflecting on his moment in sports history, he talked of a letter:

> It was an exceptional day. In particular, it was very meaningful for me to win the Masters' [sic] during Arnold Palmer's final competitive appearance here. I couldn't help but think back to the letter he wrote to me after the 2002 Bay Hill Invitational. "You never would have won as many tournaments as you have by playing a more conservative game," he wrote. "Keep playing to win. Keep charging. Your majors will come."[4]

———◇◇◇◇———

A letter's impact almost always exceeds the writer's effort. Once when the sister of a friend of mine was in prison, I took five minutes to let her parents know I was praying for them. Within a day, the father called my friend about the "wonderful, handwritten letter." What timing, my friend said to me. Her parents were feeling so alone. The next time her father visited, he had my note with him to show her.

My love of letter writing turns on wheels large and small.

I love to order personalized stationery in sizes for any occasion or length. I love to survey and purchase postage stamps. I loved the Ronald Reagan commemorative stamps and snapped up some of the first issues. As I write this, besides presidents, a letter sender may purchase stamps of Yogi Berra, Arnold Palmer, Charles Schulz, Pete Seeger, Women's Rowing, National Marine Sanctuaries, Otters in Snow, or Women Cryptologists of World War II. (Postal tip: Stock up on the "evergreen" stamps to hedge against rate increases.)

My wife and I both descend from letter-writing stock. Before my father-in-law retired as president of A. L. Williams Insurance Company, every morning he signed hundreds of letters to individual members of his sales force—people he singled out to recognize and encourage. Most of his letters included a handwritten P.S. Many of his recipients framed the letters because words matter and words on paper matter longer. Occasions and reasons to write them abound.

The letters we write commit the stories and the people to our minds too, like these, spurring years of memories and relationships:

- A family of two girls and a father who lost their mom and wife to cancer. Having lost my father and a brother

48

at young ages, I wanted to connect with them in their grief. I wanted to assure them of my love and continued prayers.

- A high-ranking White House official serving a president I didn't vote for. Following a small West Wing meeting, the man mentioned to me the challenges of parenting an autistic child, and I wanted to encourage him. I enclosed a book by a mother of an autistic child.

- My sophomore high school history teacher. I was no fan of history, but I liked and admired *him*. I commended him for his service at that school for thirty years.

- The speaker I brought in for a company retreat, to thank him. (He told me nearly half of our staff had written him thank-yous, now in his "encouragement file.")

- A pastor friend in Florida when his first book came out. I saw it in the San Francisco airport and read it on my flight home.

- Friends on the West Coast who lost a child to leukemia—to encourage them, and to grieve with them.

- A columnist in a national magazine, thanking him for a meaningful and especially candid piece.

- A high school basketball teammate of my daughter's, discouraged about her playing time. At the next game the girl's father said, "You'll never know how much your letter meant to her."

- The pastor of a church that our son and his wife attended for a number of years. I wrote to him after our first visit. Several years later, greeting us after a service, the pastor immediately brought up my letter.

- An NCAA championship basketball coach when news of his retirement struck his legions of fans as too soon. He had coached and conducted himself with class, and I told him so.

- A senior pastor, about the associate pastor who filled in for him one Sunday. It's one thing to praise the younger pastor, another to praise him to his boss. (I wrote the associate, too.)

- Each of our grown children, frequently, for a variety of reasons, or no reason at all.

Could I say the same things in emails? Of course, but would it mean as much? I wrote to my in-laws recently when they both turned eighty in the same month. The next time I saw my mother-in-law, she told me she kept every letter I've written to them in the thirty-five years of my marriage to their daughter. I had no idea.

—◦◦◦◦◦—

In the 2008 presidential primary season, I wrote to a prominent partisan power broker, my political polar opposite, commending him for his civility on one television program after another with the spokespersons and surrogates of opposing candidates. In the coarsening world of presidential elections, I said, his tone and demeanor stood apart.

Months later, when I was planning a project promoting civility, I asked this same man by email if we could meet in person for his opinion on the idea. We didn't know each other, and I referenced the letter. The next morning came a remarkable reply: "Mark, I'd be honored to meet you. Your letter sits in a frame on a bookshelf in my office. Call my assistant and set it up."

A few weeks later I stepped into the man's office in Washington, D.C., a mini museum of framed pictures and handwritten notes, including two from American presidents. And there was my letter, just as he'd said. Hanging up the phone, my new friend gestured to his bookshelf. "That's the nicest letter I've ever received," he said.

Have you ever seen a framed email?

———◦◦◦◦◦———

John Wooden was the most successful basketball coach of all time, full stop. His record ten national championships at

UCLA will stand forever. (His runner-up, Duke coach Mike Krzyzewski, had half as many titles in twenty seasons more.) Coach Wooden died in 2010, four months shy of his one hundredth birthday. Nellie, the only love of his life, had died in 1985. After their fifty-three-year marriage, for the next twenty-five years the famously humble coach wrote to her.

In this excerpt, a sportswriter named Rick Reilly captures the depth and expression of Coach Wooden's love:

> He took me into his bedroom once, in 2000. The clocks were all wrong. He stopped them at the time of Nellie's death, 15 years before. Only one side of the bed was slept in, and above the sheet, not under them, and hadn't been since the day she died. On her pillow were hundreds of little letters in envelopes tied up in bundles of yellow ribbons. He wrote to her every month telling her how much he loved her and what all the kids were doing. Did it right up until the last few months of his life, when his eyes stopped working.[5]

―――∞◇∞―――

What's true of life is true of business. Successful executives tend to be letter writers. Once I wrote to three leaders in one company in one day, including the chair of the board. The only reply came from the highest and busiest—the chairman.

That same week I wrote to two coaches. One was a high school basketball coach; the other was Mark Richt, then the head football coach at the University of Georgia. Coach Richt wrote back to me within days, during a crucial part of his season. The other coach never wrote. When busy people make time to write letters, they make time for people, and what's more important than that?

———◦◦◦◦◦———

Late one evening I went to kiss my then sixteen-year-old daughter good night after what seemed to have been a tough day for her. I found her sitting on her bed, flipping through a box of papers.

"What's that?" I asked her.

"My letter box," she said.

I hadn't known she had a letter box. But from over her shoulder I could see one of my notes to her, and I smiled.

Chapter 7

HONESTY CAN BE COSTLY
But Telling the Truth Is Good Business

Would you want to do business with
someone 99 percent honest?
—Sid Madwed

In the fourth quarter of the year, capping an already record season, our biggest client signed a contract with us at three times the size of our largest fee ever. A cardinal rule of business is that one client must not be too much of the pie. But there we were: one signed contract, one client now representing one-third of our annual income.

Two weeks into the new era, my colleague and I put final touches on a comprehensive plan to lift our client's organization to new levels of public awareness. Media relations, events, message points, collateral materials, crisis management . . . with a lot of thought and hard work, the pieces fitted and rotated like interlocking gears. We slid the documents into our briefcases and drove to the airport.

Picture now a small conference room and the big hand on my watch straight up for our three o'clock. All that's missing is the vice president who solicited our contract. Running late, I mused, when the communications director slid something to me from across the table.

"I've been instructed to start the meeting," he said. "Why don't you begin by reading this?" I opened the folder and felt the color leave my face. This director had never supported our role in his organization. The letter in my hands called for a much-reduced agreement.

Our silent clash was not about money but philosophies. Years later I can still recite a line or two from that letter. This man resented our thinking we knew their PR needs better than they did. He wanted us to continue to write and distribute news releases and press kits but wanted none of our public relations counsel.

His letter lay open in front of me. "Your organization took forty-five days to respond to our contract," I said. "I won't respond to this letter in a forty-five-minute meeting. Let's adjourn until your vice president can join us."

When the vice president appeared at last, nothing changed but some of the fog lifted. Yes, he'd increased our responsibility and compensation. Yes, he'd signed a contract. But the director of communications wanted to reverse the decision, and he permitted it.

Between the afternoon's body slam and our late flight

home, my colleague and I deliberated in an airport lounge. This was one-third of our business. Our most obvious response was to restructure along the client's new direction and salvage a still-large piece of business. But both of us were too stunned, too fatigued to decide then.

With the dawn I knew we would resign the account. We were a public relations firm, not a news release factory. Doing and thinking are two sides of one coin. My three senior advisers supported the decision, and we took the news to the staff, though giving them the story got no easier. I choked up telling them they deserved better from this client.

No bridges were burned in our resignation letter (a few years later they rehired us), but I plead guilty to believing we were the experts in PR. Our decision point was whether to take a check at any cost, and the decision made itself. We walked away from our biggest monthly retainer ever. (Time would reveal that it made us a better company and me a stronger leader.)

———◇◇◇◇◇———

A good part of public relations is intangibles: relationships, time, experience, knowledge, creativity, instinct, ideas . . . counsel. The front end of every project is fairly standard, but no project is a formula, and no outcome, ever, is a promise.

Factor in a client's "wish bias," and a gap opens between client expectations and seasoned PR counsel.

We built DeMoss on giving our clients the truth, sometimes hard to receive and frequently unpleasant to deliver. Who wouldn't rather say, "Sure, we can get you on the *Today Show* and in the *New York Times*." Or "Your book is the best we've seen this year. We'll pitch it to every major national media outlet."

In the gap between wishes and reality, a PR firm has three options. First and easiest is to charge for what *might* happen and start the clock. Second is to counsel the client to change in ways to move closer to its goals. Third is to say squarely that in the absence of true news value, no firm can deliver *Good Morning America* or even a local talk show, whereupon the firm declines the work or vice versa.

A client of ours once wrote what he expected to be that year's landmark religion book. His publisher sent us the manuscript with a memo giving us first dibs to publicize and promote it, and to handle book interviews and appearances with the major national media outlets. This project was supplemental, money on top of our healthy retainer.

Problem was that the book had no mainstream news value. Unwilling to waste my client's money or jeopardize our credibility with the media, I believe I surprised the publisher by declining the work and telling him we could not meet their expectations. Within a week another firm had signed on, though predictably, the high-level publicity never came.

———◦◇◦———

Among our many successful projects, our work philosophy also cost us existing business, kept us from new business, and on more than one occasion got us fired. A national youth organization, a longtime client, wanting to appeal more directly to teens, asked us to help it rebrand. Any new brand, we said, should leap to a young person's mind—more ESPN than C-SPAN, more MTV than PBS. But the group was established; its leaders were wanting innovation without change. Within a month of our presenting to the board they let us go at significant cost to us for work already done.

An up-and-coming pastor of a large-and-growing church flew with his wife to talk PR with me. Our discussion naturally included lifestyle issues such as his plans to purchase a Rolls-Royce, something neither his wife nor I would endorse. He'd come ready to write a first month's retainer check. I suggested he wait for a proposal, which I sent a week later, and the line went dead.

A large Christian nonprofit needed a PR firm to help manage a national crisis. On the first conference call with several of its leaders, I advised financial transparency. They asked for a meeting in person at their headquarters, and we set a date. Soon after that, their office called to "postpone," and that was that.

Another client, thinking we'd failed to grasp his importance to the world, came to my office personally to say if we would concentrate on making him known, he'd pay us what our other clients were paying *combined*. He was serious enough to ask for that number, and I was honest enough to tell him it didn't matter.

The money my firm lost in telling the truth was considerable, and would have made a difference for an agency our size, but at any price, honesty is a bargain.

Chapter 8

MONEY ISN'T EVERYTHING;
GOOD PEOPLE ARE
Create a Winning Corporate Culture

*You can buy a person's hands but you
can't buy his heart. His heart is where
his enthusiasm is, his loyalty is.*
—Stephen Covey

The idea came to me about twenty-five years ago, but I remember as if it were yesterday the mental conflict that came with it. I was the young president of a relatively new firm with the uncommon idea to reward good work with no work. My hardworking and most-senior colleague's five-year mark was on the horizon. Why not preempt any hint of burnout by giving her paid leave—a sabbatical? And why not make that five-year reward standard company policy?

The dissenter in my head ended every sentence with a question mark. Could a company of eight or ten people afford to give up a key person even for a few weeks? What about clients depending on her service and counsel? What if, during her time away, she decided to change companies or careers? What if more and more employees began to qualify? What then? Maybe there's a good reason so few companies offer that kind of time off.

I told myself that the risks of offering a sabbatical fell far below the risk of a valued employee feeling wrung out and unappreciated. If one person's absence could jeopardize our entire operation, I reasoned, we had bigger problems than paid time off. I thought of the pleasure of telling a faithful worker to cap years of effort by refueling her personal interests and then coming back to us. Someone with a recharge was more likely to stay a second five.

With a bit of fanfare I introduced the company to the DeMoss sabbatical plan. After five years of service, any employee of any rank (companies that offer sabbaticals often limit them to executives) was entitled to four consecutive weeks of paid leave with the option to attach another week of regular vacation. We'd reimburse up to $2,500 in travel costs.

We meant business. Anyone on sabbatical was fully extracted from all firm work. No checking email or voicemail. No calls for any reason from fellow employees. No business or professional requirement such as reading or taking an educational course. I asked only that the person taking a sabbatical commit to at least one more year with us.

Beth used her time off to hike the north coast of Maine,

visit family and friends in North Carolina and Virginia, and do nothing at all. In four weeks we spoke not once. To my delight, the wheels of the firm rolled on; the rest of our team ably covered Beth's client work, knowing others would follow suit when it came time for their sabbaticals.

Just as sweet was Beth's summary statement: "The timing was impeccable. You'll never know," she said, blowing in with fresh winds and new energy. She thanked me as if I was teaching her that like a car too long in city traffic, a person needs to flush the mental buildup. In truth, little information existed back then for or against business sabbaticals. Logic alone says loyalty runs two ways, an employee giving her best deserves my best in return. Or as Einstein put it, a person doesn't need rest so much as variety.

After Beth's policy-pioneering trip to northern Maine, more than two dozen people in our small company earned and took sabbaticals. One spent five weeks exploring Australia, having planned only a week of his trip before heading out. Then came the second wave of DeMoss sabbaticals, a direct result of the first. Ten years' service met with six weeks of paid leave, a $10,000 bonus, and a weeklong, all-expenses-paid trip for two to any Ritz-Carlton hotel or resort in North America. Beth was also the first of five to earn our fifteen-year sabbatical.

Extravagant? Not if you're also reading between the lines, where it says that treatment of your people trumps client service, schedules, output, and spreadsheets. Happy employees affect, or infect, every other aspect of business. Also between the lines, read in all caps that a company's policy has to be more than talk.

To the list of anemic business phrases like "committed to excellence" and "high-quality"—website words unattached to company policy—I would add, "People are our best asset." Maybe half of working Americans are satisfied with their job. Far fewer are "very satisfied." Roughly 40 percent of American workers feel disconnected from their employers; two-thirds spend their days unmotivated by their employers' business goals or objectives; some 25 percent admit to showing up just to collect a paycheck.

My journey from essentially autonomous PR consultant to the head of a PR firm was paved with human insights. Chief among them was that good people—trusted, professional, respected, inspired, rested people—*are* the firm. From the start I sought out first-rate employees and then sought to keep them. Money motivates less than some might think. When a great employee gave his notice to move his family back to his favorite state, a key client urged me to stoke the employee's income, a strong vote of confidence for the employee, to be sure, but personal decisions ultimately have no price.

DeMoss paid competitively, but some of our employees left higher-paying jobs to join us. And though every decision has its intangibles, I believe a choice of where to work comes down to four motivators.

The first is mission. Communications professionals wanting to advance the work of faith-based organizations and causes generally loved our work. All honest work glorifies God, but some employees came to us needing more sense of mission than promoting grocery store grand openings and hotel conference facilities.

The second motivator is a good leader. Not the smartest or brightest necessarily—I'm grateful for that—but a leader fixed on mission and committed to the people with him. I learned to weigh my company's every move against its potential effect on our employees. Some years I paid myself less money because people serve the leaders who serve them.

Third is corporate culture, that unwritten code for work environment, people chemistry, traditions, management style—even dress. Corporate culture determines whether the employee spends her energy looking out for her turf or helping the entire group gain new ground.

We worked in a class-A office tower with a view from our tenth-floor space that on a clear day stretched for twenty miles. Why not save money in a single-story commercial complex? Because all of us, collectively, willingly, shaved profit-sharing for surroundings that also gave energy, fostered creativity, stimulated good thinking—a place we were proud to share with clients and guests. In that spirit we valued annual fall retreats for all staff and spouses, Monday morning devotional time, and our café with its stunning city views.

The warp and woof of the DeMoss culture were collaboration and teamwork. We preached and practiced open-door management. We commemorated victories together and learned from moments that hurt. When conflicts came, as they did, each person's value was a given. Over the years word filtered back to us that our former employees attested to the special corporate culture.

I said earlier that money is less a motivator than some might imagine, and though it can't match mission, leadership, and culture, it is a factor. The fourth motivator is compensation and benefits: salary, health insurance, retirement plans, vacation schedules, and other perks. Most of our competitive benefits came together in an employee committee that didn't include me. Our employees designed our menu-style benefits program. They all belonged to an annual profit-sharing pool (also minus me), a tangible reward for hard work, good attitude, and solid results.

According to a Gallup study we were in a small minority (21 percent) of American workplaces where employees were "engaged"—passionately and profoundly connected.[1] My response to the report was less pride for us than sadness for the majority of workers unable to associate eight-plus hours a day with personal meaning, much less joy.

My personal picture of love of work is a man named Willie who cleaned shoes, picked up towels, and greeted everyone entering the locker room at Augusta National Golf

Club. Any job at Augusta National beats almost any other golf club job anywhere, but Willie was still a breed apart. I met him when my college-age son and I got to spend two days on the hallowed grounds of Augusta. In a locker room steeped in history, when I asked Willie how long he'd worked there, he tilted his head upward and said, "I've *logged* thirty years, but I haven't *worked* a day."

One year an employee satisfaction ranking put DeMoss at number eight in the *Atlanta Business Chronicle*'s survey of Atlanta's A+ Employers (fewer than one hundred employees). Every year we participated, the Best Christian Workplaces Institute (with *CT* Magazine and the Christian Management Association) ranked us first in companies under ninety employees. Clients and organizations came to us with questions about our sabbatical program and our corporate culture.

Great companies, I'm convinced, operate on gratitude. For my money, the best case study for keeping my best employees began with the nerve-racking decision to show our gratitude by letting them walk out the door. Because good people aren't just the main thing in a business. They're *everything*.

One postscript, if I may. Michelle was with DeMoss for fifteen years when she died unexpectedly. Our plane to her funeral service was about to take off when a text came to me from a veteran journalist at one of the nation's largest newspapers. "Please know the culture you created, which I experienced primarily through Michelle, changed the world," it said. "Crying at my desk over the loss."

Did our money-isn't-everything culture really change the world? Not by a long shot. But it made a difference in the life of this journalist.

Chapter 9

EVERYONE'S IN PR
Do You Practice It Poorly or Well?

Everything you do or say is public relations.
—Anonymous

Name someone, *anyone*, not in public relations, and whoever you come up with, I challenge it. Because no one, anywhere, ever, is *not* in PR. Without saying a word, every person, you included, is a mouthpiece, a critic, a supporter, a case in point, an endorsement, an argument, a walking billboard, a testament for or against . . . something. *Everyone* is in PR.

Most people shy from the PR label, and given certain ideas about it, it's no wonder. On the most cursory level, PR is a communications profession. Dive into slang, and it gets a little beat-up with tags like *spin, party line, propaganda, fluff, sizzle*—or worse—all meaning the opposite of the truth or the facts. Public relations practitioners also get pinned with *flack, hack, slippery,* or *slick*.

The professional world of PR is fairly small, interestingly. The PR Council, the only U.S.-based association dedicated to PR agencies, is but 130 members. The industry's accrediting agency, the considerably larger Public Relations Society of America, has thirty thousand individual members in a hundred or so local chapters. The small world of paid PR professionals notwithstanding, the *function* of PR is universal. That's what I want to address.

As a thirty-year resident of Atlanta, I most often fly Delta Airlines, headquartered here and serving everywhere. One way and another, Delta dominates my region. Like most companies of any size, it has an executive to represent it to the public—a "PR guy." Its guy is Senior Vice President and Chief Marketing and Communications Officer Tim Mapes. He and his team are Delta's official voice to the world.

Some world. Last year, 200 million passengers flew Delta from 275 cities across six continents. By the day, business travelers, vacationers, families, and anyone with a ticket and a photo ID filled seats on nearly four thousand Delta flights. Not one passenger among the millions, I'd wager, would recognize Mr. Mapes the "PR guy," by which I'm saying that despite his title and job description, Mr. Mapes is not the face or voice of Delta.

Nor is Delta CEO Edward Bastian. The airline's public image, its touch to the masses, is not the team in its official global PR department. For me and my fellow road warriors,

Delta is whichever of its eighty thousand employees we encounter on any given day. Delta's PR is the purview not of Tim Mapes but of every person drawing a Delta paycheck.

Do I mean to include mechanics, accountants, and support staff? I do. Each one has a spouse, parent, child, sibling, friend, or neighbor whose opinion of the airline rides on his or her relationship with the person. Multiply that phenomenon times eighty thousand and, well, we're all in PR.

I interviewed a Starbucks barista once, curious about his view of the company brand across more than thirty thousand outlets in eighty-four countries. I don't drink coffee (my wife drinks my share), but I know the Starbucks story from the book *Pour Your Heart Into It* by Howard Schultz, its first president and CEO. The young barista allowed that Schultz was the company's internal voice and face, but the brand was the frontliners, he said: him and his fellow store employees. Bingo.

I love my job. I loved our firm. I loved the staff and our work together. Most of the twenty-eight years' worth of employees at DeMoss would say it was the best place they worked, which means I did my job by them too. When we hired, when we engaged with the media, when we counseled our clients, my attitude and all employee word of mouth *was* DeMoss PR.

Big deal, you say; your field is public relations, you *should* get it right. But what about the considerable PR I practice when I have my teeth cleaned, go in for a physical, love my wife and kids, or attend church? In a given year, my personal routines signal a thumbs-up or -down for a long list of companies, organizations, people, philosophies, and beliefs for which I never see a dime.

Take my dentist—so well-oiled in his patient rotation that I'm in a dental chair, mouth open, before I can finish a magazine page in the waiting room. His respect for his time and mine so astonishes me that for two decades I've expanded his PR division with more new patients like me. (Most of his staff has been there for more than twenty-five years.)

My in-laws tipped off my wife and me to the comprehensive physicals at Executive Healthcare, part of the Emory University Hospital in Atlanta, easily mistaken for the concierge floor of a nice hotel. April and I valet park and enter through a comfortable office separate from the vast hospital system. No waiting, no lines. We complete a battery of tests never far from our doctor's full attention. And you know the refrain: I refer my friends and acquaintances.

At home I'm a PR guy for my family—April, our three children and their spouses, and our grandchildren. April and I love each other; anyone who knows us knows that. We enjoy each other's company. We're crazy about our Georgia, Mookie, and Madison, and their Scott, Betsy, and Brad—and their children. No family is perfect, but they're the best thing going. So while marriage and family often get bad PR, among the people who know us, both institutions get five stars.

As for my extended family, a biblical proverb says that "a good name is to be more desired than great wealth" (22:1 NASB). When my father died in 1979, the name he left me was mine to lose. My actions and reputation reflect on the family name. My son's will do the same.

Chick-fil-A founder Truett Cathy lived out this proverb. He amassed great wealth, but when he died at age 93, at his instructions his tombstone bears the words of Proverbs 22:1.

By contrast, my "ouch" file includes a clip about a large national conference that drew tens of thousands of people and millions of dollars to its host city. Regrettably, it was a Christian event. I say "regrettably" because of a letter to the editor about the event.

"I have worked in a downtown hotel for fifteen years," a man wrote to the major local newspaper. "Year after year, the people who attend [this conference] are the rudest people who ever come to this city." Did the conference sponsor have a PR team? It did. But official events and PR statements crumble before one personal experience. To the locals and the merchants in the host city, every conference attendee *was* Christianity.

No man is an island, the poet wrote. The Bible says we do not live unto ourselves (Romans 14:7). How quickly, how easily we inhale judgments from the people around us. In the many roles we assume each day, to be wise we also must steward our offhand power to damage or bless.

When we smile or don't smile, when we tip or hold a door, let a car ahead of us in traffic, speak to the hostess, the desk clerk, the flight attendant, the waiter who got our order wrong . . . we brand ourselves, our values, our beliefs, our employer, the church we attend, and more. Strangers around us are making real-time judgments.

We can think twice, no, *three* times, before being openly critical, or rude, or angry, or uncivil. In the work God gives us, we can treat every person with dignity and respect, regardless of station or of our potential benefit. *Imago dei.* Every person bears the image of God.

Let us stay keenly aware of the ripple effects of just being ourselves. For good and bad, we're all in PR.

Chapter 10

And Another Thing . . .
A Few More Thoughts

Do what you do so well that they will want
to see it again and bring their friends.
—Walt Disney

Wisdom rarely comes on tap. Most often it's available by the eyedropper or thimbleful, in a remark, an aside just as easily missed. In writing this book and musing over the comments and counsel that have steered my life, some of what came to mind filled chapters, albeit small ones. Others are of the thimbleful variety. A few of those I offer here.

Good Customer Service Costs Almost Nothing

Late at night in our room at a Ritz-Carlton, my wife and I stared into the dark as a construction crew down the hall hammered and drilled hour after hour. The next morning at checkout I mentioned the noise, and our desk attendant apologized. Any hotel would do that. But without consulting a supervisor or higher-up, she also gave us a complimentary night at the Ritz, something almost no hotel will do.

The gratis stay was good for that hotel only, and we've had no reason to return, so the gesture in this case cost them nothing. And yet, years and years later, in terms of my esteem, that clerk's spontaneous grace continues to pay dividends. I think I know why Ritz-Carlton is the gold standard in the hospitality industry.

At the other end of the service curve is an experience so bad I'm still writing about it nearly thirty years later. I'd walked into a national computer retail chain near my office to buy ten laptops of a certain model. After a few moments of looking, I asked the customer service rep to unlock the anti-theft bar so I could judge the computer's size and heft, and he said no.

No?

"Sorry," he said. "The computers stay locked."

He could stand next to me, I told him, while I held the computer.

"The anti-theft bar stays down."

"Look," I said agreeably, "I want to buy ten of these for my company. But I'm not spending that kind of money unless I can actually hold the computer."

Looking somewhere past my head, the young man said he had no key to the bar, and he repeated the store policy.

I asked to see the manager.

"He can't open it either."

"Let me get this straight," I said. "I came here to buy ten laptops, but you won't let me hold even a single display model?"

"That's right," he said with the authority of a security guard at the Guggenheim. I turned toward the front door and then pivoted back.

"You know what amazes me?" I said. "You seem as if you don't care whether or not I buy ten computers."

The gap between a five-star hotel and a computer super-store was not amenities, prices, or inventory. It was the sense of its fundamental values. You can say the hotel pays better than the computer store, but an employee's spirit turns on more than a paycheck. In one case, a clerk's human concern turned a bad night into an endorsement. In the other, a fundamental absence of customer service turned a sure sale into bad PR.

Four Powerful Phrases

When my children were little, I taught them that words have powers. "Stupid" and "shut up" close doors. "Please" and "thank you" open them. As my kids grew and moved into the world, I taught them a few phrases that, in my experience, can unbolt shut doors, leave open doors ajar, and cut passages in solid rock.

"IN MY OPINION"

My field is public relations, my role is to dispense counsel, but the advice I give most often comes down to my opinion, and I tell my clients that. I wish we heard those words more often from our governmental leaders, but I hope you always hear them from me.

Does "in my opinion" imply weakness? On the contrary, in my opinion it speaks strength: "For what I'm about to say, I take full responsibility." That's confidence signaling and listeners take their cues. The more certain I am, the more likely I am to preface or conclude my saying so with "in my opinion."

"WHAT DO YOU THINK?"

The greatest business textbook ever written includes a proverb that says, "Where there is no counsel, the people fall; but in the multitude of counselors there is safety" (Proverbs 11:14 NKJV). The best counsel givers are counsel seekers.

In the course of a public relations career my judgment and decisions have been colored by relevant input from employees, friends, industry peers, my wife—and by counsel less obviously relevant. Only arrogance would reject advice because of a person's job title.

At the same time, in work with several hundred organizations, I have seen leaders make major decrees or decisions with no more than a counsel of one. A leader can do that;

he or she ultimately makes the final judgment. But to form that judgment with no outside information, news, opinions, experience . . . without knowing the dissenting side . . . well, the wisdom of one is wisdom at a deficit.

"LET ME ASK YOU A QUESTION"

The stupidity of people comes from having an answer to everything. The wisdom of the novel comes from having a question for everything.

Award-winning Czechoslovakian author Milan Kundera drew back the curtain on the power of his writing when he said he doesn't tell, he asks. "It seems to me that all over the world people nowadays prefer to judge rather than to understand, to answer rather than to ask," he said, "so that the voice of the novel can hardly be heard over the noisy foolishness of human certainties."[1]

It's also said that knowledge has right answers and wisdom has right questions. So let me ask: Do you employ the power of a question?

Humanly speaking, it's all but impossible to ignore a good question. Just the phrase "Let me ask you . . ." hooks us. Try it in your next meeting. Used wisely (not to manipulate), a question is your passage to new information, to time to think, and to the regard of your listeners. In our culture, questions show interest; they flatter. In the lifespan of my firm I saw good questions sharpen my employees' thinking. We're all better for the ask.

"I DON'T KNOW"

When Billy Graham turned seventy years old, *Newsweek* asked him why, given his public influence, he never ran for political office. Mr. Graham said he wasn't smart enough. An attorney, brilliant in his specialty, has said he chose his branch of the law because he was no good at the others. Both men are exceptions.

Great men and women, accomplished artists, gifted leaders who are confident in their strengths are equally confident about their weaknesses. Show me an expert able to say, "I don't know," and I'll show you a constituency who trusts what she *does* know.

I'm not for a string of shrugs, needless ignorance, or lack of preparation. I'm suggesting that along with phrases in the spirit of "In my opinion," "What do you think?" and "Let me ask" is the confidence-spreading habit of refusing to blow smoke. Most people able to say "I don't know" usually know more than the "knowers."

One of the best things leaders can do for their children, spouses, employees, clients, and anyone else is to make it okay to not know. Where honest seeking is welcome, people are more likely to collaborate—to suggest crazy ideas, think out loud, and get to information no know-it-all can come up with alone.

Small acts of humility can work to great effect. Think like a customer. Admit ignorance. Ask for help. Take a look around. Then join the smart minority who know they don't know everything and continue to learn.

—————— PART 2 ——————

Wisdom for Your Personal Life

For wisdom is better than jewels, and all that you may desire cannot compare with her.
—Proverbs 8:11 (ESV)

Chapter 11

GOD OWNS IT ALL
A Wise Perspective on Things

*Most human beings have an almost infinite
capacity for taking things for granted.*
—Aldous Huxley

I will never forget the Labor Day weekend at 2 A.M., on the lawn in my pajamas, watching with my family as flames gutted our English Tudor to a stone shell. By dawn, everything we owned was lump or ash.

I was ten years old, the first to escape the inferno. My family told me I sleepwalked down the stairs to the outside. A fireman saw me shivering and wrapped me in a blanket while a policeman coaxed my sister to jump from a second-floor window into his arms. The scene was surreal: quiet and chaotic, lonely and crowded.

For the next week we lived with friends, then we bought school clothes and rented a house for nine months before moving again. I shake my head to think that long before home fire alarms were standard, all nine of us awoke from deep sleep and escaped virtually unharmed.

Years later on Halloween night, my friend Bruce and his wife took their kids through our neighborhood while Bruce's father-in-law stayed behind to pass out candy. Bruce and his family returned to find their home ablaze, too late to save the children's grandfather. The next day I walked around the charred lot with Bruce, the smell of sodden ashes taking me back to my own memories.

Insurance policies replace bricks and furniture, and people can rebuild, but no policy can replace the things that bear family value over market value.

Haiti was the poorest nation in the Western Hemisphere on January 12, 2010, when a 7.0 magnitude earthquake swallowed millions of tons of steel and concrete, killing more than two hundred thousand people, most of them already subsisting on less than two dollars a day. Haiti's strongest earthquake since 1770 left a third of its ten million residents in dire need of emergency aid. My visit there on the first anniversary of the quake impressed on me again that we *own* nothing.

Any given day's news of war, calamities, disease, and death should convince us that personal ownership is fleeting. To the degree that we accept that, our lives have considerably less surprise and stress. To the degree that we fight it, our possessions own us.

In August of 2005 a Category 5 hurricane hit a level-three levee, flooding death across New Orleans and the U.S. Gulf Coast. Katrina was the costliest U.S. hurricane since 1851 and its fourth deadliest, claiming eighteen hundred lives, displacing a million more and racking up $180 billion in damage.

In the early days after Katrina, I twice visited the devastation. In Shreveport, Louisiana, I toured a large basketball arena converted into a makeshift shelter for hundreds of uprooted families. Franklin Graham's Samaritan's Purse relief organization had sped emergency supplies and transitional housing to the region. Together we walked up and down rows of cots, listening, talking, praying with people who lost everything.

Many of the cots had Bibles on them. Many of the Bibles were in use. Now and again, we'd hear, "At least we're alive." "God has us." "The stuff doesn't matter." We'd come to encourage and left with a truer bead on where our treasures lie.

The following March, I toured St. Bernard Parish and the Lower Ninth Ward, again with Franklin and this time also with his father, Billy Graham. Two hundred churches had asked the two men to hold a "Celebration of Hope." Before the event, up one deserted street and down another we crisscrossed neighborhoods erased by the mighty Mississippi and Lake Pontchartrain.

A long block inland from the Industrial Canal, blocks from where President George W. Bush had toured a few hours earlier, we climbed out of our vehicle to walk at the intersection of Forstall and Galvez Streets. Nearby we could hear the incessant clanging of steel beams being driven deep into the ground to erect new levees. From the small crowd of media that met us there, a journalist shouted out. "Mr. Graham, what can we learn from Katrina?" Without missing a beat, the eighty-seven-year-old evangelist answered, "That there's more to life than material things."

Unless that's true, hundreds of thousands of storm victims had no reason to face another day. But they did, and they do. Triumph over adversity is the American story.

Leave the Gulf Coast to travel the nation, and that truth disappears again under piles of *stuff*: stock portfolios, multiple mortgages, cars and technology, all the right plastic cards. We rent space to store the excess. When parents and grandparents die, we contest the wills and jockey for more.

The American Dream tripped and face-planted in March 2009 when Bernie Madoff pled guilty to the richest Ponzi scheme in U.S. history. The thirty-seven thousand trusting souls who lost the $65 billion in his care included Madoff's sister, Sondra. Her brother's 150-year prison sentence was no help now to her or to people like sixty-six-year-old retired consultant Miriam Siegman, going from a financial backstop to food stamps. "He took everything," she said. "I still have the rest of my life to live, or try to live, in incredible stress and total poverty."

"Hurricane Madoff" tore through the personal fortune of Elie Wiesel and took $15 million of his foundation's assets. The Nobel Laureate and Holocaust survivor noted how many of Madoff's clients were left with nothing, having entrusted their life savings to "a man they thought was God."

Madoff would finally admit that since 1991 he had made not one legitimate investment with his clients' money. All of it went directly into his personal business account. And then, in 2021, the man who lived in a penthouse on the Upper East Side of Manhattan and owned multiple homes, died in a federal prison, estranged from what was left of his family. Peter Madoff, who spent forty years working for his brother and, ironically, was the company's chief compliance officer, served nine years in prison for his role in the scam. Madoff's eldest son, Mark, was found dead in his $6 million SoHo apartment, hanging from a black dog leash. His brother, Andrew, died in 2014 of a rare lymphoma.

A small Old Testament book known simply by the name Job tells the story of "the greatest man among all the people of the East" (Job 1:3 NIV), a desert magnate with seven sons and three daughters, seven thousand sheep, three thousand camels, five hundred oxen, five hundred donkeys, and an army of servants. Satan singled out Job for affliction, and God permitted Satan to have everything but Job's life.

Bandits, fire, hurricane, and disease took Job's family, herds, land, and health. As bad news and more bad news blew in with every new messenger, Job murmured: "Naked I came from my mother's womb, and naked shall I return. The LORD gave and the LORD has taken away; blessed be the name of the LORD" (Job 1:21 ESV). The next verse says: "In all this, Job did not sin or charge God with wrong."

King Solomon wrote in Ecclesiastes, "When God gives someone wealth and possessions, and the ability to enjoy them, to accept their lot and be happy in their toil—this is a gift of God" (5:19 NIV).

My life is blessed. I've had a successful career, the rare gifts of a wife and a good marriage, three children I admire, two sons-in-law and a daughter-in-law who multiply our joy, five beautiful grandchildren, and good health—even after a bout with cancer. I've had a dream house and more possessions than I need or deserve. Amid all this, to try to stay conscious of God's full ownership does several things in me.

First, it makes me thankful to the Creator who owes me nothing yet gives me everything. What can I have but gratitude? Second, it gives me purpose. In the way money managers invest and oversee the resources in their care, God has made me a steward, a fiduciary mandated to invest prudently, spend wisely, and waste nothing. Third, it opens my hands and loosens my grip on *stuff*. "How much should I give?" gives way to "How much should I *keep*?"

That night on the lawn with my brothers and sisters, watching every earthly possession waft into flames and smoke, of course we grieved. The speed and scope of the damage at first left us dazed. But my father's practice of giving away more than he kept had filtered into our DNA and sharpened our instincts about *things*.

Too bad about the house, but it was never really ours.

Chapter 12

THE WISDOM OF FIRSTS
The First Hour, the First Day, the First Dime

I feel it is far better to begin with God,
to see His face first, to get my soul near
Him before it is near another.
—E. M. Bounds

My father was the most successful man I ever knew. Unrelated to how I viewed him, his genius in direct-response marketing of individual life and health insurance formed the National Liberty Corporation, with its five companies and subsidiaries. The little business that started at the kitchen table, by the time of his death twenty years later, was the largest mass marketer of individual life and health insurance in the world.

To what did my father attribute his success? Enough people must have asked him that he committed it to paper in a booklet he titled *God's Secret of Success*. Since his death, that vest-pocket treatise, long out of print, has played large in lives around the world. If I were to give you its contents right here, you might say: "That's *it*?" But if you were to practice the points, to weave them into your life, eventually you'd be amazed that they had ever seemed small.

The First Hour of the Day

Art DeMoss believed the gate to success swung open first thing in the morning, in the day's uncluttered hour, when he talked with God in prayer and listened to God as he read the Bible. Some people will give this tip a double take. The head of a booming corporation didn't check in first on morning news? In those days that was the newspaper, but my father didn't take it. Maybe TV while he got dressed? Nope. Remember, no TV set in the DeMoss home. What about the stock market, just a glance? No, again. Because as sure as he brushed his teeth and ate breakfast, Dad started his day with God.

"It should be our rule never to see the face of men before first seeing the face of God," said Charles Spurgeon, the great nineteenth-century British preacher. Only a fool would fail to post a guard on the gate of the day. "The morning watch anchors the soul so that it will not very readily drift far away from God during the day," he wrote. "He who rushes from his bed to his business without first spending time with God is as foolish as though he had not washed or dressed, and as unwise as one dashing to battle without arms or armor."[1]

Dad died more than forty years ago, but to this day one of my clearest memories of him is his morning routine. By example he paved the path to my similar habit now, though I admit to less than a full hour each day.

If you're thinking you could just as easily spend time alone with God in the noon hour, you're right, you could—unless something else comes up. You could do it in the evening before bed, assuming you still have energy and focus. You could hope to steal a few moments throughout the day. We can all hope for a lot of things. But nothing sets the day like matching our best hour to our deepest and dearest Resource.

Spending our first moments with our Creator is more practical than legalistic. It's the only time we can truly protect. When that time is hectic with children or work or similar busyness, we can set an alarm a little bit ahead. I'm convinced the person who does this has an advantage over those who don't.

The First Day of the Week

Besides the first hour of the day, my father gave God the first day of the week. Now that we blur Sunday with Saturday or any other workday, respect for the Sabbath seems, well, extreme, dated, obsolete. And it may be. If hours in the day are no more than measurable productivity units, then one of the world's richest men is right. "Just in terms of allocation of time resources, religion is not very efficient," Bill Gates says. "There is a lot more I could be doing on a Sunday morning."[2]

The lengths of the wording of the individual Ten Commandments intrigues me. Most are brief—four to ten words. "You shall not kill." "You shall not lie," and so on. Then comes the ninety-four-word instruction to keep the Sabbath day holy. Who can say that God devoted more words to the fourth commandment for emphasis, but who can deny that a day of rest hits reset on our minds, bodies, work, and personal relationships?

Chick-fil-A founder Truett Cathy was a Sabbath keeper. If you're a patron of the wildly popular restaurants he founded, you know that come Sunday you get your chicken somewhere else. Come Sunday, every one of the twenty-nine hundred Chick-fil-As in forty-eight states is shut tight, potentially costing the family-owned business more than $3 billion a year. If you'd asked Mr. Cathy why, he'd have turned to the subject of devotion. "Closing our business on the Lord's Day is our way of honoring God and showing loyalty to Him," he'd say. "My brother Ben and I closed our first restaurant on the first Sunday after we opened in 1946, and my children have committed to closing our restaurants on Sundays long after I'm gone."

My Sundays are hardly one sustained act of prayer and meditation, but neither are they a checklist of paying bills, work, emails, or prep for Monday. Sundays tend to be slower and quieter—good days to work on this book, but I didn't. I try not to travel on Sundays, but when I'm out of town on the first day of the week, regardless of how little sleep I got the night before, I want to be in church and otherwise do as little as possible. In my life, at least, Sunday rest correlates to weekday productivity.

Plenty of people have to work on Sundays. Nurses, pilots, hotel workers, cooks, waiters, public-safety workers, to name a few. Dad wrote, and I write, to those of us who *can* set the Sabbath aside but don't. As for what constitutes work on a Sunday, I came across a pretty simple definition: *Decide what's work for you, and don't do it.*

"Hurry," said philosopher Dallas Willard, "is the great enemy of spiritual life."[3] God Himself offers promises for those who honor "His Day":

> If you watch your step on the Sabbath and don't use my holy day for personal advantage, if you treat the Sabbath as a day of joy, God's holy day as a celebration, if you honor it by refusing 'business as usual,' making money, running here and there—then you'll be free to enjoy God! Oh, I'll make you ride high and soar above it all. I'll make you feast on the inheritance of your ancestor Jacob. Yes! God says so!
>
> —Isaiah 58:13–14 (THE MESSAGE)

The First Dime of Every Dollar

Now for the success secret so personal and so often misapplied that some of my readers may consider it in poor taste to bring up: My father gave the first part of every dollar to God. The concept, also known as tithing, was not invented by modern televangelists. It is at least as old as the early Old Testament. Jesus endorsed it as an act of love, and certainly a gift of our resources is a regular and potent reminder of the Source of all we have.

"Honor the LORD with your wealth, with the firstfruits of all your crops," King Solomon advised. "Then your barns will be filled to overflowing, and your vats will brim over with new wine" (Proverbs 3:9–10 NIV).

For whatever reason, even most churchgoers overlook or outright avoid this wise principle. Evangelical giving these days averages 3.2 percent of their income—less than the percentage in 1933, during the Great Depression. Last year one in five churchgoers gave nothing at all. And then there's John D. Rockefeller, the Standard Oil founder who died in 1937 having given away today's equivalent of ten billion dollars. Of course, you say, Rockefeller was one of the richest men of all time. But his giving started when every penny counted:

> I had to begin work as a small boy to support my mother.
> My first wages amounted to $1.50 per week. The first

week after I went to work, I took the $1.50 home to my mother. She held it in her lap and explained to me that she would be happy if I would give a tenth of it to the Lord. I did, and from that week until this day, I have tithed every dollar God has entrusted to me. And I want to say that if I had not tithed the first dollar I made, I would not have tithed the first million dollars I made.[4]

There's George Jenkins—"Mr. George" to Publix Supermarket employees—who lived from 1907 to 1996. The employee-owned, privately held corporation he founded currently sells $48 billion in its thirteen hundred stores. In his final interview, a reporter asked him what he thought he'd be worth if he hadn't given so much away. Mr. George said, "Probably nothing."[5]

No giver can outgive God. We're told to bring our tithes into the storehouse, followed by, "'Test Me in this,' says the Lord Almighty, 'and see if I will not throw open the floodgates of heaven and pour out so much blessing that there will not be room enough to store it'" (Malachi 3:10 NIV). It's true we don't "give to get." It's also true that God says He will give when we do.

My father's respect for giving sailed well beyond his days. In his will he directed the vast majority of his assets and holdings to a charitable foundation dedicated to telling others the good news of God's love, a decision I never questioned or resented.

In his little booklet, *God's Secret of Success*, Dad urges us to put God first in our habits and first in our homes. Success is a byproduct of first things getting top priority, he says over and over, a truth you can't know until you try.

So try it. First for a morning, then every morning for a week, and every week for a year. Observe the Sabbath. Give the first of everything you receive and everything you are. See if you don't also have the secret of success.

Chapter 13

A Turtle on a Fencepost
Acknowledging How You Got Where You Are

> *We don't accomplish anything in this world*
> *alone . . . and whatever happens is the result*
> *of the whole tapestry of one's life and all*
> *the weavings of individual threads from*
> *one to another that creates something.*
> —Sandra Day O'Connor

A businessman named Allan Emery drove to Boston's Logan Airport to pick up an accomplished and well-known pastor flying in from Pittsburgh. By every standard the pastor was impressive, but the person least impressed seemed to be the pastor himself, which impressed Emery. "He seemed to see himself as a spectator to what God was doing," Emery recalled. When Emery credited his passenger with at least some of his church's sizable achievements, the pastor shrugged.

"Allan," he said, "when I was a schoolboy, from time to

time we'd see a turtle on a fencepost, and every time we did, we knew it didn't get there by itself."

Later when Emery wrote a book about lessons he picked up in his life, he entitled it *A Turtle on a Fencepost*.[1] Since I first heard the term, I've loved how deftly it undercuts the "pull yourself up by your bootstraps" American myth—as realistic as a turtle on a fencepost claiming to be self-perched.

Tiger Woods was the first athlete ever to earn $1 billion. Announcers rhapsodize over his talent and his work ethic, which are epic. Even so, Tiger didn't swing to the top on his own, and he knows it.

He began as a blank page, Tiger says in *How I Play Golf.* "Through my first teacher, my dad, the page began to fill. Pop gave me many great lessons, not only about golf, but also about life." When interviewers ask him to credit his success, Tiger names early teachers like Rudy Duran, John Anselmo, Jay Brunza, and Butch Harmon (longest and perhaps best-known). He shares the spotlight with longtime caddy Steve Williams "at my side through many tough rounds and great moments."[2]

Every professional golfer begins as a junior golfer, and junior golfers, as my son, Mookie, would attest, are multi-dependent—driven to tournaments, followed for hours on the courses, fed, coached, taught, filmed, analyzed, encouraged, and consoled. Parental scholarships cover lessons, clubs, balls, club dues, and greens fees. Long before battalions of popular support showed up, Tiger Woods and similar rock-star golfers relied on the unmerited, inexplicable, and divine graces of coordination and physical ability. (While it takes a team to rise, stars fall on their own, as Tiger's reckless personal behavior also reminds us.)

———◦◇◦———

Team. Team. Team. Ever hear of Juan Carlos Ferrero? Juanjo Moreno? How about Alberto Molina Lopez, Alberto Lledo, Alex Sanchez, Fran Rubio, or Juan Jose Lopez? They're the team that took tennis phenom Carlos Alcaraz to the top of last year's U.S. Open, making him the youngest World No. 1 in two decades, at nineteen years, four months, and six days old.

Coach Juan Carlos Ferrero, a former World No. 1, runs the Equelite Tennis Academy in Spain, where he first spied the thirteen-year-old Alcaraz's raw potential, emphasis on raw. "When he arrived at the academy he was a noodle," Coach Ferrero says. "He was quick, but he didn't have muscles."

Fitness coaches Alberto Lleda and Alex Sanchez and physician Dr. Juan Jose Lopez helped Alcaraz survive the higher levels of play and then excel. Juanjo Moreno and Fran

Rubio serve as physiotherapists. Alberto Molena, Alcaraz's agent since he was thirteen, connects him with blue-chip sponsors like Nike and Rolex. The 2022 U.S. Open champion is old enough to know he soared to first place from one hundred twentieth in the world on many wings not his own.

———◇◇◇◇◇———

Heisman Trophy winner Steve Spurrier is also a national championship football coach, one of four people in the College Football Hall of Fame as both a player and a coach. For years he voted in the *USA Today* Coaches' Poll, and for years he gave a vote to Duke University in the preseason poll. Duke is a basketball power but a pushover in football. No other coach in the poll had time for the Blue Devils, but Coach Spurrier saw to it that Duke started every football season with one vote.

The story is that Coach Spurrier, retired since 2015, is a man with a long memory and a healthy sense of gratitude: "Duke University hired me twice when I didn't have a job, 1980 and 1987, so I owe a lot to Duke University."[3] When Georgia Tech released Spurrier as quarterbacks coach in 1980, Duke brought him aboard as offensive coordinator, his springboard to the professional ranks. When he wanted to return to the college game after three seasons as head coach of the USFL's Tampa Bay Bandits, Mississippi State and Louisiana State passed him over, but Duke gave him another shot—this time as head coach. Two years and two ACC Coach of the Year titles later, Coach Spurrier took a call from his alma mater to coach the Florida Gators for a wildly successful twelve-year run. He coached ten more years at the University of South Carolina, and still he never forgot Duke.

———◆———

From sports to children's television, though Fred Rogers of *Mr. Rogers' Neighborhood* died twenty years ago, his life on and off his award-winning show of thirty-three years still helps children and parents navigate life—and to appreciate the people in our lives. In 1997, at age 68, when he was honored with a Lifetime Achievement Emmy award, Mr. Rogers beautifully, characteristically, captured the essence of a turtle on a fencepost.

"So many people have helped me to come to this night," he said. "Some of you are here, some of you are far away, some are even in heaven. All of us have special ones who have loved us into being. Would you just take, along with me, ten seconds, to think of the people who have helped you become who you are? Those who have cared about you, and wanted what was best for you in life. Ten seconds of silence—I'll watch the time."

In the quiet, a room of adults in tuxedos and gowns

wiped away tears. "Whoever you've been thinking about," Mr. Rogers said, ending the pause, "how pleased they must be to know the difference you feel they've made." Then he thanked the people he'd been thinking of.[4]

———◇◇◇◇◇———

Through my twenty-eight years at the head of my firm, a long list of people at home or on the job either "loved me into being" or filled out the team that drove our success. I may have been a self-starter, but I am not self-made. My Creator endowed me with certain abilities, instincts, characteristics, and strengths. Then came my parents, teachers, coaches, advisers, clients, staff, friends, books, my wonderful wife, and my children. Who are we but the sum of the many who got us here?

When this book was first published, my wife had beautiful stationery cards designed for me with a turtle on a fencepost. I have two sets of turtle cufflinks. The turtle was not designed as a beauty detail, but he beautifully reminds me of why I am who I am.

Just after David was made king of Israel, when God promised him that his name would be "like the names of the greatest men on earth," David prayed these words:

"Who am I, Sovereign LORD, and what is my family, that you have brought me this far? . . . . There is no one like you, and there is no God but you. Do as you promised, so that your name will be great forever. Then people will say, 'The LORD Almighty is God over Israel!'" (2 Samuel 7:18, 22, 25–26 NIV).

From the fencepost, amen.

Chapter 14

THERE ARE NO DEGREES OF INTEGRITY
You Either Have It or You Don't

*If you have integrity, nothing else matters. If
you don't have integrity, nothing else matters.*
—Alan K. Simpson

The Coronavirus pandemic of 2020 was a hardship for most people, a tragedy for many, and, for a handful of opportunists, it was shooting ducks in a barrel. By 2022, the U.S. Department of Justice charged forty-eight people with bilking a collective $240 million from the government for meals not served to children who did not exist. Prosecutors called it the largest fraud in any pandemic-relief program.

In one year pandemic-related white-collar crimes opened thirty-nine thousand Department of Labor investigations. The Small Business Administration still has fifty agents sorting through two million possible fraudulent loan applications.

Corruption clearly isn't confined to pandemics. In an unrelated case dripping with irony, former Detroit Police

Lt. John F. Kennedy pleaded guilty in federal court to conspiring with another city police officer to take bribes in connection with a towing scandal. Kennedy previously headed the police department's Integrity Unit.

In finance, Ernst & Young—global powerhouse corporate auditors—paid a $100 million fine for widespread cheating on their employees' ethics exams. Fraud from the "gatekeepers within the gatekeeper," the SEC's enforcement division director called it, cheating "by the very professionals responsible for catching cheating."[1]

The world of academics suffered the "Varsity Blues" college-admissions scandal. Celebrities, actors, and titans of industry paid a total $25 million to secure stand-ins to take their children's college entrance exams, to falsify applications, to bribe college officials to get into elite universities like Georgetown, Stanford, Southern California, and Yale. Mastermind Rick Singer admits he "unethically facilitated college admission" for children in more than 750 families, and for his trouble faces three and a half years in prison and a fine of $19 million.[2]

The scope and the names take your breath away. Parents at the top of their fields, advisors like Singer, elite college coaches, school administrators . . . in an unseen network of greed and lies. Morrie Tobin, a Los Angeles businessman, told authorities the Yale women's soccer coach wanted $450,000 to help Tobin's daughter get into the school. One

"Eliza" Bass got accepted to Tulane, Georgetown, and Loyola Marymount as an "African-American tennis whiz, ranked in the Top 10 in California," except that "Eliza" was white and didn't play tennis.

America's pastime let us down, too. After years of wallowing in averageness, the Houston Astros beat the Los Angeles Dodgers in the 2017 World Series. By 2019 a published story linked the Astros to an elaborate centerfield-camera system to steal signs from opposing catchers and pitchers. Houston won the World Series again in 2022, but under a cloud of suspicion and disgust. The team paid a $5 million fine; two managers were suspended and then fired. But the damage exceeds the penalties.

In California, a Stanford dropout named Elizabeth Holmes founded a company called Theranos to produce a machine, or so she claimed, able to run thousands of diagnostic tests on just a few drops of blood. It would revolutionize healthcare. From Hollywood and Wall Street, from the worlds of science and medicine to the U.S. government, influencers in the highest echelons served on Elizabeth's board and poured millions of dollars into her scheme. Theranos was valued at $4.5 billion until a company insider and a *Wall Street Journal* reporter blew the lid off its lies and the dangers to patients. In 2022, Elizabeth Holmes, then married and pregnant, was sentenced to eleven years in prison for fraud.

In a sad twist of irony, the book that inspired me to write

this book was later exposed for flagrant plagiarism. William Swanson was CEO of Raytheon, a defense contractor with eighty thousand employees and $22 billion in annual sales. In 2004 he published *Swanson's Unwritten Rules of Management*. Major corporations responded by giving away hundreds of thousands of copies.

Until someone noticed that sixteen of Swanson's thirty-three rules had appeared first, verbatim, in the late W. J. King's 1944 booklet *The Unwritten Laws of Engineering*. Swanson's board of directors docked his pay a million dollars, but no amount can buy back a man's name or a corporation's stature. (In the "birds of a feather" column, Swanson's predecessor as CEO settled with the SEC for accounting irregularities.)

———◇———

"So-and-So has a lot of integrity," someone will say, but by definition "a lot of integrity" is impossible. *Integrity* means "complete," from the Latin *integritas* for "whole." It means all or nothing, yes or no, full or empty, but not how little or how much. Integrity has no sliding scale.

Before any of us smugly put ourselves above the headliner frauds, keep in mind that soul fragmentation comes in every size. A man who says he's working late when he's dining with a female colleague is not whole. Nor is the account exec padding billable hours. Or the woman returning for a full refund on clothes she's worn. (The industry term is "wardrobing," costing retailers $12.6 billion a year.) Fragmentation begins in white lies, in a few dollars' difference, in "just-this-once" compromises. The alternative is to try to "always do right," which, according to Mark Twain, "will gratify some people and astonish the rest."

The point isn't to be infallible. The point is to know how fallible we are and use the wall that protects, the glue that binds, the compass that guides. "He who is enslaved to the compass," as someone has said, "has the freedom of the seas."

At Harvard University's John F. Kennedy School of Government, the Center for Leadership publishes an annual National Leadership Index. One standout year respondents said they wanted a leader to be upright; 95 percent put "honesty and integrity" ahead of a leader's ability to speak, give orders, cooperate with others . . . or intelligence, open-mindedness, vision, or decision making.[3]

"Would you choose a financial services company for strong ethics or for high returns?" another survey asked a thousand Americans. Nine hundred fifty chose strong ethics.

How is it, then, that we will destroy in moments the reputations of a lifetime? Part of the answer, I think, is that while an actual collapse may take moments, the process of getting there tends to be long and slow—like termites, like a mouse gnawing a net. Not until the tower topples or the bottom drops out do we see what small things ultimately become our undoing.

———❊———

Karl Eller pioneered outdoor advertising. He founded Clear Channel, in fact, a $2.7 billion conglomerate operating in fifty countries. A member of the Advertising Hall of Fame, Eller died in 2019 at age 90. At the University of Arizona Eller College of Management, some of his philosophies are etched in stone, and a couple of examples show why:

> Without integrity, motivation is dangerous; without motivation, capacity is impotent; without capacity, understanding is limited; without understanding, knowledge is meaningless; without knowledge, experience is blind. Experience is easy to provide and quickly put to good use by people with the other qualities. Make integrity the compass that guides you in everything you do. And surround yourself only with people of integrity.[4]

In his book *Integrity Is All You've Got*, Eller says the one constant in his varied career is how integrity works in people's lives: "Those who have it usually succeed; those who don't usually fail," he says, and he'd know. When he was sixty-five years old and $100 million in debt, he refused to file personal bankruptcy, gradually repaying every dollar. "My integrity became my collateral," he says in retrospect, which explains why so many of his creditors were willing to wait. "And," he adds, "why other people lent me money to finance a new enterprise."[5]

———◦◦◦◦———

Another important story belongs to Huntsman Chemical Chairman Jon Huntsman, which he tells best:

In 1986, after lengthy negotiations with Emerson Kampen, chairman and CEO of Great Lakes Chemical Company, we agreed he would purchase 40 percent of a division of my company for $54 million. Negotiations had been long and arduous, but a handshake sealed the deal.

I didn't hear from Kampen for several months. Approximately four months after those discussions, Great Lakes lawyers called to say they would like to draft some documents. They had been dragging their feet—business as usual. It took three months for this rather simple purchase agreement to be placed on paper. The time lapse between the handshake and the documents was now six and a half months.

In the interim, the price of raw materials had decreased substantially, and our profit margins were reaching all-time highs. Profits had tripled in that half year. Nothing had been signed with Great Lakes and no documents had been exchanged. Kampen called with a remarkable proposal.

"Forty percent of Huntsman Chemical today is worth $250 million, according to my bankers," said Kampen. "You and I shook hands and agreed on a $54 million price over six months ago." Although he did not think he should have to pay the full difference, he thought it only fair that he pay at least half and offered to do so.

My answer was no, it would not be fair to use the appreciated value, nor should he have to split the difference.

He and I shook hands and made an agreement at $54 million, I said, and that's exactly the price at which our attorneys would draft the documents.

"But that's not fair to you," Kampen responded. "You negotiate for your company, Emerson, and let me negotiate for mine," was my response.[6]

Huntsman could have taken more money with no sense of compromise, but his word was his integrity. The next part of his story hits me right between the eyes:

Kampen never forgot that handshake. He took it with him to his grave. At his funeral, he had prearranged for two

111

principal speakers: Governor Evan Bayh (now in private business) of Indiana and me. I never was personally close to Emerson, but he and I both knew that a valuable lesson had been taught. Even though I could have forced Great Lakes to pay an extra $200 million for that 40 percent ownership stake in my company, I never had to wrestle with my conscience or to look over my shoulder. My word was my bond.[7]

Integrity isn't what we do when it serves us. It's who we are even when it seems to work against us. It's who we are in the dark and how we treat people when there's no benefit to us. If forced to choose, I would hold to integrity over intelligence, wealth, talent, popularity, or any brand of success. Integrity can never be taken from a person; it can only be handed away. Or as Job said, "Till I die I will not put away my integrity from me" (Job 27:5 NKJV).

A closing story. Cecil "Red" Brenton was known to Toronto motorists as the "Christian mechanic" because of an investigative newspaper story. In 1972, a reporter from the *Toronto Star* went to thirteen automobile garages with a car in perfect condition except for a loose spark plug wire. Garage after garage, mechanic after mechanic gave him a false diagnosis and charged him to fix it. Mr. Brenton found the loose wire and fixed it at no charge. When the reporter asked him why, he said, "I'm a Christian." The story ran in the paper and drivers flocked to Mr. Brenton's service station, where he worked another dozen years before retiring.

Twenty-one years after the newspaper piece, Cecil Brenton died from prostate cancer and Hodgkin's lymphoma. The *Toronto Star* reported his passing not with the usual obituary, but in a standalone article under the headline *"Cecil Brenton, 89: 'Christian mechanic' known for integrity."*

I use these stories because they're known, but at the end of the day public attention for being good or bad is not the point. A person *can* cut corners, grift a bit . . . get by, maybe, with a certain amount or level of fraud. But as an African American professor once said about a matter that the law would allow but his conscience would not: "When the book is opened, I know where I want my name."

Chapter 15

A Proverb a Day
*Wisdom for Every Aspect of Your
Life, in One Short Book*

*Nothing ever becomes real until it is
experienced. Even a proverb is no proverb
to you till your life has illustrated it.*
—John Keats, letter to George and Georgiana Keats

Two prostitutes approached the king's bench. The first had given birth to a baby boy, and three days later, in the same house, the second gave birth to a baby boy. During the night, the second woman rolled over and accidentally smothered her newborn. What did she do? She switched infants. The next morning the first prostitute awoke to a dead child and the other woman claiming her live child.

"She's lying!" the second prostitute shouted. "Her baby is dead! This baby belongs to me!"

A court hearing circa 900 BCE predates DNA testing, and the king had a long docket. He asked to have a sword brought to him, and an aide produced a blade. Gesturing, the king said: "Cut the child in two and give each mother half."

"No!" the first mother cried out, "give the baby to her!"

"Fine!" the second one yelled, "no one gets him!"

"The first woman is the mother," the king said. "Give her the baby."

The monarch whose reputation for wisdom was sealed that day was Solomon, son of David, Israel's first king, and David's wife Bathsheba. Toward the beginning of his forty-year reign, Solomon collected wise sayings and pored over them. At some point he winnowed the riches into a book in the Bible's Old Testament under the simple name Proverbs. From nearly a thousand years before Christ, Proverbs is one of the earliest examples of wisdom literature, a priceless guide still widely considered the gold standard of counsel.

Of the Bible's sixty-six books, to my thinking, Proverbs is the most provocative. Two dozen centuries before Sigmund Freud and psychological profiling, thirty-one short chapters penetrate human nature with insights into sex, anger management, slander, wealth, welfare, business ethics, intoxication, pride, and fissures in character as relevant as tomorrow's top trending topic.

Proverb is a Hebrew word meaning "to rule or to govern." Much of it has to do with self-mastery, and the only thing better than reading it is reading it routinely. If you were to take in a chapter a day, in one year you'd have twelve readings of a book that I consider boredom-proof. After nearly four hundred trips through the entire book, I still rely on it for new insights, reminders of timeless truths, and life-guiding principles.

Billy Graham said he read five psalms a day "for getting along with God," and a chapter of Proverbs a day "for getting along with my fellow man." In my growing-up years, I saw my father do the same thing. He also read every year through the Old and New Testaments, still another reminder that a mind and character cannot be left to chance.

To sample Proverbs, flip around. Just don't be deceived by the simplicity. A proverb is an acorn with a tree inside—a puzzle piece to character—and character, in the words of Pulitzer Prize–winning historian Barbara Tuchman, is destiny.

Here's my sample for you, from the NKJV translation (italics added):

Proverbs 1:33: *"But whoever listens to me will dwell safely, and will be secure, without fear of evil."* If we listen to it, wisdom will protect us.

Proverbs 2:11: *"Discretion will preserve you; understanding will keep you."* Like an invisible shield, good judgment deflects problems before they can strike and destroy.

Proverbs 4:25: *"Let your eyes look straight ahead, and your eyelids look right before you."* Life's highway is lined with wrong exits, fake billboards, flashing arrows, and wreckage. A farsighted driving instructor warns us to keep our eyes on the road.

Proverbs 5:21: *"For the ways of man are before the eyes of the* LORD, *and He ponders all his paths."* We can lie to ourselves. We can lie to the IRS, our spouses, coworkers, neighbors, bosses, personal trainers, and the guy who mows the lawn. God reads us straight through.

Proverbs 6:27–29: *"Can a man take fire to his bosom, and his clothes not be burned? Can one walk on hot coals, and his feet not be seared? So is he who goes in to his neighbor's wife; whoever touches her shall not be innocent."* Enough said.

Proverbs 8:11: *"For wisdom is better than rubies, and all the things one may desire cannot be compared with her."* Wisdom is the ace in every play. Nothing comes close.

Proverbs 10:19: *"In the multitude of words sin is not lacking, but he who restrains his lips is wise."* The difference between speaking words or withholding them can be the difference between sin and wisdom.

Proverbs 12:1: *"Whoever loves instruction loves knowledge, but he who hates correction is stupid."* Your critics have information that your friends are withholding. If you love the truth and want to grow, the people who correct you have the goods.

Proverbs 15:1: *"A soft answer turns away wrath, but a harsh word stirs up anger."* Most arguments begin with tone of voice. If your first reaction to a tone is anger, wait for your second reaction and soften your tone. Even if you have to fake it, soften it and feel your temperature cool.

Proverbs 16:18: *"Pride goes before destruction, and a haughty spirit before a fall."* A triumphant general entering Rome is said to have paid an attendant to walk alongside and whisper in his ear, "You are but mortal." When delusions of grandeur threaten your grip on reality, repeat as often as needed: "There is a God, and it's not me." The fifth verse of this chapter says, *"Everyone proud in heart is an abomination to the LORD."* Everyone. And *"Though they join forces, none will go unpunished."* None.

Proverbs 19:17: *"He who has pity on the poor lends to the LORD, and He will pay back what he has given."* Think of it: when we give to the poor we lend to the Lord, and He repays us.

Proverbs 20:18: *"Plans are established by counsel; by wise counsel wage war."* The advice on seeking advice is to do it. Before you lay out a project, consult the veterans.

Proverbs 22:1: *"A good name is to be chosen rather than great riches."* A certain celebrity cleaned up from a drug habit and the life that went with it. Years later when he was falsely accused of something else, the court of public opinion knew his record and believed the worst. It's easier to restore a life than a name.

Proverbs 24:17–18: *"Do not rejoice when your enemy falls, and do not let your heart be glad when he stumbles lest the LORD see it, and it displease Him."* Take the high road and let God take care of our enemies.

Proverbs 26:4: *"Do not answer a fool according to his folly, lest you also be like him."* The next time someone baits you, overreacts, boasts, or is patently outrageous, do nothing. Relax into the silence. Self-restraint won't get you hits on social media, but it will steer you past senseless exchanges.

Proverbs 28:6: *"Better is the poor man who walks in his integrity than one perverse in his ways, though he be rich."* They're not mutually exclusive, but given a choice between wealth and integrity, choose the latter.

Proverbs 31:10: *"Who can find a virtuous wife? For her worth is far above rubies."* The image of a rare jewel reminds young men of what to look for in a life mate and older men of the priceless fortunes in wives of noble character.

I hated having to edit this list, by the way. The point is to read the entire textbook.

A single chapter in Proverbs averages thirty verses and five minutes of reading time. I can't predict how much wiser you'll be for making it a daily habit. I can guarantee you'll be wiser for it than using the same minutes to scroll through Instagram, Twitter, or TikTok. "Blessed is the man who listens to me, watching daily at my gates, waiting at the posts of my doors," Solomon writes of wisdom. "For whoever finds me finds life, and obtains favor from the LORD" (Proverbs 8:34–35 NKJV).

One morning when April was running late, she saw me sit down and open my Bible. "Read me whatever you're reading," she said. Turning to that day's chapter in Proverbs, I saw a subheading. "It's about 'The Crafty Harlot,'" I said. "You still want to hear it?"

"No," she said, "but I want *you* to hear it. Go ahead!"

I get these flashing warning lights every month, and I welcome them.

I'll close with an endorsement. My son, Mookie, is in his thirties now. On the morning of his graduation from high school, he left a priceless note on my desk with a final line that still makes my eyes sting: "I've been reading a chapter of Proverbs every day since eighth grade because of you."

I hadn't known he was doing that. The habit came from his father, who got it from his grandfather, whom he never met. Three millennia after the book's first publication, Solomon was right again: "A wise son makes a father glad" (Proverbs 15:20 NKJV).

Chapter 16

THE WISDOM OF AGE
Seek Out Older People

Knowledge in youth is wisdom in age.
—Ancient proverb

The Ryder Cup is one of the greatest events in all of sports. Every second year, for three days, America's top twelve golfers face off against Europe's twelve best in a *team* competition, a departure from golf's schedule of individual-play tournaments.

In 2006, the U.S. Ryder Cup captain was top-ranked golfer Tom Lehman, who knew a lot about golf and precious little about team sports. So he sought out the master, the "Wizard of Westwood," the ninety-five-year-old John Wooden, former longtime coach of UCLA basketball, winner of an unprecedented ten national championships. (That's twice as many as legendary Duke Coach Mike Krzyzewski. No active college coach has won more than two.)

Impressive, you say, but still, why would a forty-seven-year-old golfer want advice from a coach, in an unrelated sport, twice his age, whose last game was thirty years earlier?

Easy answer: because Coach Wooden had what Lehman lacked. Lehman excelled in an individual sport. Coach Wooden was first and last about the sum of his players. Photos in Coach's apartment might show players alone and in groups, but Coach himself only appeared with the full team.

When Coach Wooden heard from Lehman that the U.S. Ryder Cup contenders mostly practice alone, his first line of advice was to keep the golfers together. Lehman said U.S. teams repeatedly failed to live up to high expectations, and Coach dismissed it. "I never dealt with expectations," he said. "Our team never talked about winning."

At one point in the conversation, from a near-century of living above reproach, Coach Wooden said, "Don't be concerned about your image and your reputation. That's who people think you are. The only thing that matters is your character, who you really are on the inside; focus on that, be more concerned about that."[1]

A story is told about Coach Wooden and a certain all-American center who arrived for his first day of basketball practice flouting the team rule against facial hair. Coach Wooden told him to shave, and the towering star athlete told the coach no one had the right to tell him how to wear his hair.

Coach Wooden said, "You're right, Bill, I don't have that right. But if you don't shave, we're gonna miss you."

Sitting across from Coach Wooden now, Lehman had to ask: Would he really have let Bill Walton go? The ultimatum, was he serious?

"Dead serious," Coach said. "Rules are for everyone or they're no good."[2]

———◇◇◇◇———

Going now from slam dunks, national championships, and notoriety to the school my kids all attended, Lamar Lussi never coached a team or taught a class but his influence on generations of lives would fill a book. I first met Mr. Lussi when he was head of the school's janitorial and transportation staff. Now he's the school's official Director of Encouragement, his unofficial role all along.

What can a ninety-year-old man do for kids a sliver of his age? Big things in small ways. For as long as we've known him, Mr. Lussi has telephoned every student on his or her birthday with congratulations and a personal prayer. (Usually it's the first call of the day. He's called our home at 6:45 A.M.) Kids remember that.

Mr. Lussi has called as far away as Iraq to encourage former schoolboys and schoolgirls serving in the armed forces. His investments in their lives end not when they graduate but when they marry or turn twenty-five and take on their own responsibilities for next generations.

Anyone with a calendar and a phone list could do what Mr. Lussi does, but no one else could be Mr. Lussi. To a student struggling, he is a sympathetic ear over lunch. To a patient in a hospital or a family in the waiting room, he is a comforting presence. He drove to Florida unannounced once to wait with the parents and siblings of a young man in cancer surgery. Another time the Director of Encouragement was the only non-family member to visit a young student's grandfather in the hospital. At an age when most people no longer drive, Mr. Lussi logs hundreds of miles a month to hospitals and funerals for students and their parents—even after his wife's passing in 2021.

Thirty years my senior, Lamar Lussi personifies the high call of service, and the lesson comes home to the people he serves. "He's a pillar here," the school's headmaster told the local newspaper. "I've never met anybody like him," my son said in the same story. "He's just the most encouraging man in the world."

—⁂—

Three of my grandparents were gone before I was born. My mother's mother passed away when I was young. Yet as far back as I can remember, interesting adults have filled my life.

Dinner hours in my parents' home served up missionary stories, business strategies, political philosophy—topics easily sparked among active minds and lives. The DeMoss dining room table was my first brush with the Greatest Generation.

As a high school student, I intuitively bypassed the church youth group for a Sunday morning men's class where a businessman probably four times my age taught through the entire Bible every year. His insights fell on me like sun and rain on a new plant. I couldn't have said what drove me, but I gravitated toward wisdom, toward people decades ahead of me on life's road.

———⋈———

As I begin my seventh decade, I understand—no, I envy— Tom Lehman's visit with John Wooden. Men like Coach Wooden and Lamar Lussi prove again that we are better for our time under life's tall and rooted trees. We seize the moments with them where we find them. Some like Mr. Lussi are known to a relative few. Others are national presences, like Coach Wooden and the late Jerry Falwell Sr.

When my father died at age fifty-three, Mr. Falwell was forty-six years old, a public figure, and among the first visitors to our home. A week later he was back with us to participate in Dad's memorial service. He later spoke at my brother's memorial service and co-officiated at my wedding.

When I enrolled at Liberty University, the school Mr. Falwell founded in Virginia's Blue Ridge Mountains, the Falwell home was as good as mine. After graduation, for eight years, I worked closely with Mr. Falwell, managing his office, traveling with him several hundred thousand miles a year. Yes, he was controversial, but from thousands of hours observing him off stage—in the rear of a plane, in an office, in a hotel room, in his home—I saw firsthand the truth he lived so vigorously: namely that people matter most.

After services, this Virginia preacher was notorious for being the last person to leave, staying to shake hands, to listen to anyone and everyone who wanted his ear. He did it when he was out of state too, knowing it would delay his return home. Through five decades of public ministry, Jerry Falwell conducted virtually every wedding and funeral asked of him, often multiple ceremonies in a day. Nurses and doctors at Lynchburg's two hospitals knew him from the rounds he made several times a week for more than fifty years. The people he served never forgot it.

Jerry showed me that people are important and that family is most important. From my near-total control of his calendar and schedule, I knew nothing took priority over his wife, daughter, and two sons. Or his wife's brother and his children. Or her sisters or parents. Family birthdays, even for grown-ups, trumped invitations to the White House, or to appear on *Nightline* or *Larry King Live*, or to go anywhere else. I learned priorities from someone who had them in good order; those eight years in the company of a man almost my dad's age made me a better husband and father. (My friend died at seventy-three in 2007 as this book was first published.)

———⚬⚬⚬———

Bill Bright, who died in 2003 at age eighty-one, was a presence in my life for so long I can't remember not knowing him. "Uncle" Bill traveled the world at the helm of the organization he and his wife, Vonette, founded in 1951 on the campus of UCLA, and he often stayed in our home.

By the time of his death, Campus Crusade for Christ (since renamed Cru) amounted to twenty-seven thousand full-time staff members in one hundred ninety countries, most of those staff members raising their own financial support. The organization's *JESUS* film is the most widely translated film in history, shown in more than one thousand languages to billions of people. More than two billion copies of Mr. Bright's little booklet, *The Four Spiritual Laws,* have been distributed around the world.

Bill Bright taught me to think big and to never stop thinking. Even as he was dying from pulmonary fibrosis, he was dreaming, planning, and writing. In his final five weeks he wrote me three letters, each one a gem. His son mailed the last one to me after his death. The letters mention initiatives near launch and writing projects near completion. With his signature passion, he encouraged me to use my life to help tell more people that God loves them. Bill Bright was a states-man in a world with too few statesmen. His vision, focus, and gentle spirit enriched every part of my life.

———⟨∞⟩———

Sam Rutigliano was 1980 NFL Coach of the Year when he led the Cleveland Browns to the AFC Central Division championship. Four short years later, after a 12–9 loss to the rival Cincinnati Bengals, he was shown the door. Like most coaches, Sam had valleys on the field and off, but he was who he was in large part because eighteen years earlier he had made it through his lowest point.

Sam and his wife, Barbara, and their four-and-a-half-year-old daughter, Nancy, drove away at midnight from Sam's brother's house in Montreal to get back to a summer camp in Maine where they were working. Sometime early that morning, Sam woke up off a road near Berlin, New Hampshire. Little Nancy was dead, pinned under the wheel of their toppled Volkswagen. Nothing else in his life could rival that pain, certainly not being fired by the Cleveland Browns.

After eleven years with various teams, six more with the Browns, three with ABC Sports and ESPN as an analyst,

Rutigliano came to Liberty University to build a Division I football program, no easy task. Thirty years of life separated Coach Sam and me, but we became fast friends, and I was again privileged to know a great man in his daily life.

What I saw would distill to two words—*excellence* and *class*—right down to Coach's way with the critics who circle football programs like moths on floodlights. From his years of coaching professionals, he had a way of reverse engineering to help young people start early to develop character and integrity. Through twenty-plus career moves, Sam was heralded when he won and scorned when he lost. He understood human nature. He knew that "winners make plays and losers make excuses."

A person couldn't spend time with Sam Rutigliano and not be better for it. I knew it then, and I see it still. That's not to say we can't learn from our peers, but here was a man who suffered the loss of his first child the year I was *born* and never left the often-grueling game of life.

———◇◇◇◇———

Character, servanthood, the value of staying in the Bible, the importance of the people in our lives, thinking big, managing adversity—I saw those things first in older people. From the time little feet can dangle from adult chairs at the dinner table, one of the best things we can do for our children is what my parents did for me: expose them to people whose very lives lift our line of vision.

Or put it this way: in a culture fixed on youth, when it's direction you're needing, look for someone farther down the road.

Chapter 17

Shut Up and Listen
Learn to Listen More Than You Speak

Even a fool who keeps silent is considered
wise.
—Proverbs 17:28 (esv)

In 2006, as I started work on this book, America was up to its ears in congressional hearings for Judge Samuel A. Alito—then president Bush's appointment to replace retiring U.S. Supreme Court Justice Sandra Day O'Connor. The Senate Judiciary Committee—eight Republicans and seven Democrats—would have to confirm the appointment in a formal inquiry called, ironically, a hearing. In the weeks leading to the inquisition, as reporters pressed senators for their opinions on the president's choice, invariably the answer was, "We'll have to wait to hear from the judge when he's before our committee."

The fifteen senators at Judge Alito's hearing each had thirty minutes to draw out the court appointee on any topic or issue. Regrettably for Judge Alito and the public, the fifty television cameras at the proceedings must have caused amnesia because the committee members forgot everything but their opportunity to talk.

On page one of *The New York Times* a bar chart captured the lopsided ratio between the individual senators' grandstanding and Alito's responses. Only two senators had less to say than the man they came to hear from. One pontificated to the tune of four thousand words (like reading this chapter four times over), leaving minutes to hear from the candidate for the nation's highest court. The hearings finally wound to a close, and a sad day for democracy wrote my lead for this chapter on the lost art of listening.

And painfully, predictably, this scene replays with every new Supreme Court vacancy. The honorable members of the twenty-first century Senate seem unaware of the counsel of King Solomon of approximately 950 BCE: "Let the wise listen," he said, "and add to their learning" (Proverbs 1:5 NIV).

———◦◦◇◦◦———

Larry King racked up fifty thousand radio and television interviews, more than any talk show host in history. As his twenty-five years at CNN came to a close, eight words from him in an *Esquire* interview distilled his career with a masterstroke of understatement: "I never learned anything while I was talking." Larry was eight-seven years old when he died in 2021. I'd met him several times, watched him countless times, but I couldn't have told you what he knew or how well he knew it because Larry King was about his guests and not about himself.

I contrast that with a show I watch most weekday mornings. With his co-host and regular panelists, for three hours a day the host speaks to government and business leaders from the political left and right, a motherlode of potential frontline insight. But much of the gold stays unearthed because every "question," for the host, is a chance to impress his guest with his own expertise.

Recently the show's guest was a twenty-six-year CIA veteran who'd written a book from his impressive career. True to form, the host's elaborate questions cut the guest's answering time by half, robbing viewers like me of insights on counter-terrorism and national security.

Larry King wanted to hear from his guests; this interviewer seems to want mostly to hear himself.

———◈———

As a career PR practitioner, I take seriously that talk is my stock in trade. I understand that my stock rises and falls with what I know, which requires restocking, which requires listening, which I continually must choose to do. The trick is to let the moments pass when speaking only serves my ego. Getting attention isn't power. Informed thinking, and good judgment, those things are power.

I was with a globally respected figure—a VIP, we'll say—when he met with leaders of a national organization that was launching a major new initiative. At the organization's headquarters, the president and top brass greeted and led the VIP to the building's executive conference room. The VIP was welcomed with a standing ovation and seated at the end of a long polished table.

At the other end of the table the president rose and began to speak. And speak. Like a thespian in a spotlight he held forth on his group's vision. To be sure, he was eloquent. He was in the zone. The movement his group envisioned, he said, would reach grand fruition as like-minded groups formed a coalition to span the globe.

The VIP could have helped this group span the globe, but no one asked him to. No one asked him what he thought. Any chance of that lay buried under the president's mountain of words. Who knows why he did it. Maybe it was nerves. Maybe he was high on his captive audience. Maybe years of holding forth had robbed him of the impulse ever to hold back. Whatever the case, the clock ran down and time was up.

The president escorted the VIP to his waiting car, most certain, I sensed, of his own importance. The organization had gotten an audience with a global VIP, but it never got engagement. As our car pulled away, the VIP turned to me and asked, "Who was that fellow in there doing all the talking?"

———◇◇◇———

Once when a large church found itself in a crisis about to become public, the pastor convened a conference call of his key advisers: a couple of attorneys and accountants, a few staff members, and me as PR counsel. From my hotel room in another city, I listened to voices on the phone ring out with reactions, opinions, warnings, suggestions. After everyone else weighed in, the pastor said, "Mark, you've been quiet. What do you think?"

My silence was more habit than tactic, but a habit can serve a person. My objective was not to react to limited information but to know and assess the facts. Waiting to speak afforded me time to process what I heard and to consider a response strategy—in this case to challenge most of the advice on the table.

Because what we say carries weight, but *when* we say it can add great weight.

Advice to "Shut up and listen" foils the human desire to be noticed and known, but the best habits come, I think, in resistance training. To close my mouth, to subdue myself, to hear another person—to believe that not every moment requires my input—is a muscle worth building.

Otherwise life is like . . . well, like standing on a balcony over a breathtaking panorama and using the time to record a selfie.

Chapter 18

THE BEST DEFENSE . . . IS A GOOD DEFENSE
Why I Won't Ride Alone with Another Woman

*There's one thing to be said about
inviting trouble: it generally accepts.*

—May Maloo

Habitat for Humanity is one of the nation's largest and most respected humanitarian organizations, and it shocked a nation, not to mention Habitat supporters, when it fired its founder and president of nearly thirty years. From *The New York Times* to the *Chronicle of Philanthropy*, a sea of media served up the details: Millard Fuller, seventy-year-old charismatic leader, was accused of inappropriate conduct toward a female staff member.

The group's headquarters at the time, and Millard's home, were in Americus, Georgia—about two and a half hours south of Atlanta's Hartsfield-Jackson International Airport. (Habitat now bases in Atlanta.) Whenever Millard flew out of Atlanta, his assistant would send an inquiry through the office for anyone else driving to the airport.

A ride shared was money saved and time multiplied. In the passenger seat, Millard had two more hours to read and dictate letters. Until he showed up for work, he'd typically have no idea who would drive, and the system worked until the day when the driver, and the only other person in the car, was a female employee who later accused her employer of inappropriate behavior.

Millard denied it, period. After a protracted and costly internal investigation, Habitat's board of directors, including former president Jimmy Carter, officially found "insufficient proof of inappropriate conduct." But the damage was done to a hard-earned reputation and widespread work to help people finally have their own homes.

Millard Fuller was a friend of mine. He died in 2009 at age seventy-four, and I recount his story for multiple reasons. One is that with varying degrees of accuracy it was broadcast in articles and editorials, letters to editors, websites, chat rooms, and petition campaigns. I'm hardly bringing it out of obscurity. I also believe Millard was wrongly accused.

Millard and I first met when my firm was hired by Habitat, work that ended before this story began. We were at Atlanta's Georgia Dome—now the glitzy Mercedes-Benz Stadium; Habitat had just announced a partnership with another large organization. I entered the Atlanta Falcons' locker room to a voice loudly declaring he'd been waiting to meet me, and for the next half hour, I was the most important person in the world and a friendship was sealed.

That was the Millard Fuller effect. Top that with his love of God, and you get how his life could read like a Horatio Alger story in reverse: millionaire attorney, age thirty, sells everything and commits to serving the poor. His salary from Habitat was $79,000, characteristically small compared to almost any other large nonprofit CEO—a bargain compared with his successor's $210,000. In plain language, I loved Millard. I supported him, endorsed him, and would defend him anywhere.

My third reason to use this story is to exhort any person with any level of influence to take extreme measures to protect her or his reputation, marriage, family, and work. Inconvenient? Yes. Outdated? Paranoid? Perhaps. Think what you will, but a married person is wise never to ride—or work, or travel, or dine, or do anything, really—alone with someone of the opposite sex.

Insiders and Habitat for Humanity supporters debated the charismatic leader's controversial departure. The board drew a fire of criticism for his removal. Many details no doubt remain unknown. What is known is that until he rode in a car alone with a woman who was not his wife, he was safe.

My admonition on this is more practical than puritanical. Most important, I believe it is *wise*. In a car, a restaurant, an office—a hotel elevator when possible—to shun even the appearance of blurred lines protects not just you and your reputation, but the people you love.

Once a national political candidate was accused by a staffer of spending too much time alone with a female aide, to a brief flurry of media attention. The candidate denied wrongdoing, but he couldn't deny the facts or the poor judgment, and the coverage is forever a google away. In the valley of the shadow of the appearance of impropriety a man's reputation, his family, his campaign, his staff, and his future, took a real hit.

Why risk it? In the twenty-first century, compromising situations attract litigation and media the way rancid food draws rats. Public figures know that. They choose open-eyed whether or not to live so that a charge of bad behavior would surface more allegations or only rouse defenders. If someone accused me of a dalliance, I'd like to think a host of friends and colleagues would dismiss it with, "Impossible! He's never alone with anyone but April!"

My firm was still in its infancy—an admin assistant, a client-service exec, and me—when Beth left television news

141

to head our media relations work. In Beth's world female reporters on assignment with cameramen were as common as out-of-town client meetings were in my world. She and I needed a plan.

My informal manifesto to our first woman executive ran something like this: "We will never be alone with the door closed. If at the end of a day we are the last two in the office, one of us goes home. No lunches or dinners alone together. No shared rides to the airport; no seats together on a flight" (forfeiting potentially valuable pre-meeting time). "Out of town we'll rent two cars," I said. "Our client will reimburse us for one. My firm will pay for the other."

That kick-off conversation with Beth soon became the firm's formal policy, and though not everyone embraced it right away, to my knowledge no one questioned its wisdom. Over the years a number of clients asked for copies.

———◦◦◦◦◦———

The bigger the target, the more the shooters. I can't overstate that, and I continue to be amazed at the public figures who live as if it doesn't mean them. Once at a large religious convention in a major city, I arranged to meet a potential client, a man well-known in certain circles, in his hotel suite. I walked off the elevator, followed a long dark hall to his suite number, knocked on the door, and was surprised to be greeted by his female colleague.

Like many suites in convention hotels, this one was set up for business. The sitting area had light snacks, a dining table and chairs, a bathroom, and an adjoining bedroom. The colleagues introduced themselves to me, and we talked business. When I left the suite, the door closed behind me, leaving two people vulnerable and many more people potentially curious. I'm certain nothing was afoot, but I'm certain also that if someone had questioned the situation, these people's defense would have been Swiss cheese.

It is impossible to be physically involved with someone you're never alone with. That's a fact. There are ways to stumble besides extramarital sex, and we're all capable of every sin, so all the more reason to construct protective barricades on the riskiest terrain.

———◇◇◇◇◇———

A prominent pastor was accused of crossing boundaries with female colleagues, and I was summoned to a church where the open social culture made my company's policies look draconian. One day a key leader in the church asked me what guidelines I would suggest, and I broached the kinds of precautions I advise in this chapter. Sensing how regressive they sounded to him, I found myself holding back the words, "Listen, I'm not the one in trouble here!" This congregation was paying me handsomely to resolve troubles that at one time were entirely preventable.

The otherwise impressive leader resigned days before he likely would have been removed from the church that he had founded and given his life to. And self-restraint continues to draw mostly bad press. Since this book's last printing, former U.S. vice president Mike Pence drew new attention to the "Billy Graham Rule" to never be alone with any woman but his wife, and outrage (and ridicule) hit the fan. Professional women argued, understandably, that the practice gives an unfair advantage to their male counterparts.

Two thoughts on that. First, steps to prevent slip-ups and accusations protect more than the people at the table or in the hotel meeting room. Spouses don't have to wonder whether a professional lunch turned personal. Women in the office—and their spouses—will see that lines protect as well as divide. Second, from nearly thirty years at the head of a firm of mostly women, I can attest that no career rose or fell on private lunches with me. Anything to the contrary is lousy leadership, which is another conversation.

As for mocking the precautions, too many organizations with budgets in the tens of millions, and into the billions, have lost or fired leaders at great financial cost and long-term damage. If those organizations and ousted leaders could hit rewind now, I suspect no one would mind looking a little "neanderthal."

God built and blessed us with physical appetites and desires. He knows how easily, particularly on low days, a person can take a shortcut to a good feeling. When He commanded us to avoid even the appearance of sin He was saying *don't do this to yourself.* He's closer to us than we are to ourselves and loves us more than we love ourselves. We can trust that in His lexicon *don't* is a positive word.

Yes, the effort to avoid even a hint of indiscretion is inconvenient. So is damage control with the public, and so is the deeper damage to the people you love. Choose your inconvenience.

This comes from a PR practitioner of forty-plus years, a man acquainted with tragedy and needless damage. If you're in the public eye, live as if you know it. If you're not in the public eye, manage your conduct as if you were. *Take the extra steps.* For reasons that transcend a feeling, an emotion, or a circumstance—for yourself and for the people you love—do what it takes to help you *not* stumble . . . or even appear to.

Chapter 19

HERE'S TO NOT DRINKING AT ALL
Are Wisdom and Alcohol a Good Mix?

One of the reasons I don't drink is that I want
to know when I'm having a good time.
—Lady Astor

John was eight years old when he had his first beer and hardly older when he acquired a taste for his parents' homemade wine. Then came Jack Daniel's, his father's favorite. John tasted his first Tennessee whiskey at his sister's wedding, when he was fourteen.

John grew up to be John Daly, one of the most exciting professional golfers of the nineties and into the two thousands. (He now plays on the PGA Tour Champions for golfers aged fifty and above.) His muscular, fluid swing rocketed balls down the fairways and out of sight. His galleries rivaled Tiger Woods'. To his electrified crowds, "Long John" Daly was a cult hero for the common man.

But little about John Daly was common. In 1991, at age

twenty-five, he won the PGA Championship, one of golf's four "majors." Pundits said he lacked the control over power and distance to do it, but in four short years he won his second major at the Open Championship on the famed Old Course in St. Andrews, Scotland. John Daly was on top of the golf world, and he deserved to be.

That was in 1995. By the PGA's 2000 season a fan looking for John Daly would have to scroll down the world golf rankings to No. 507. Off the course, he'd sunk three marriages. His fourth wife was indicted in a Mississippi federal court on drug and illegal gambling charges. His gambling losses ran between $40 and $50 million. (Imagine not knowing which.) He'd lost a blue-chip list of corporate sponsors and spent at least two extended stays in alcohol rehab clinics.

After one of John's attempts to sober up, *Golf World* magazine asked him if he intended to avoid the kinds of situations that had gotten him there—the kind that can litter a man's trail with divorce, debt, and wrecked hotel rooms. "Honestly?" he said. "Probably not. I want to gamble, and I want to have a few drinks now and then. Basically, [trying to stay sober] had taken over my life, and I was miserable . . . there's no way I'd never drink again."[1]

Minus the notoriety and the size of the debts, one part of John Daly's story repeats itself in homes across America, and that's the point of this chapter. This is a book, not a sermon, so setting aside all morality, religion, or judgment and focusing solely on *wisdom*, I believe a case exists for not drinking at all.

I've never tasted alcohol, but this is not a moral argument against it. My wife and I have far more friends who drink than don't. Nor is this a biblical prescription for abstinence. (Arguably, except for kings, princes, and priests, the Bible prohibits intoxication, not alcohol.) My case isn't that drinking is wrong, but that *not* drinking is wise.

Now, scores of my friends, like millions of people, drink without excess, problem, or incident. Many who drink successfully protect themselves and others from harm or compromise, and I'm glad for that. A pastor and author who grew up in a home of teetotalers has said when he made his own decision on alcohol he set a single-drink limit regardless of the setting. There's wisdom in that, too.

For drinkers with less internal control, the data tell a sobering story:

- Alcohol is the third-leading cause of *preventable* deaths in the U.S.
- Though drunk driving deaths are down 50 percent since 1982, since 2018 another person dies at the hands of a driver under the influence every fifty minutes.
- More than 65 million Americans reported binge drinking within a month of being surveyed.

- 15.1 million adults in the U.S. over age eighteen have an alcohol use disorder (AUD).
- Alcohol is a "major contributor" to more than 200 diseases and injury-related health conditions.[2]

———⌘———

On May 25, 1979, American Airlines Flight 191 from Chicago to Los Angeles was less than a mile from its departure runway when the left engine of the DC-10 detached from its wing. The plane crashed in minutes, killing all two hundred fifty-eight passengers and thirteen crew members aboard and two people on the ground—the deadliest aviation accident in U.S. history.

The National Transportation Safety Board immediately launched an investigation, determining that the left engine was damaged in an earlier engine change in Tulsa, Oklahoma. Two weeks later the Federal Aviation Administration grounded all DC-10s under its jurisdiction and banned foreign DC-10s from U.S. airspace. A safety panel under the National Academy of Sciences convened to assess the DC-10 design and evaluate the U.S. regulatory system.

Now imagine a commercial airliner crash and two hundred seventy-three people dead not once every four decades, but every eight *days*. In 2020 alone, the National Highway

Safety Administration reported 11,654 alcohol-related traffic fatalities—the equivalent of forty-two packed jet airliners downed every year with no survivors.

If a commercial airliner crashed every eight days in the U.S., our sharpest minds would race to stop the crashes and stem the loss of lives. Leaders in government and industry, regulatory agencies, victims' groups, the law, the nonprofit sector, and the media would demand reform *now*.

And yet the daily havoc of alcohol appears to have the last word; our collective wisdom appears to be impotent. The two-thirds of Americans who imbibe appear to expect to beat the odds by drinking "responsibly," and while most of them do, many do not; probably because as one doctor put it to a national television audience: "Under the influence of alcohol, it's impossible to act responsibly."

—⚬⚬⚬—

Alcohol misuse costs the U.S. an estimated $249 *billion* a year, says the National Institute on Alcohol Abuse and Alcoholism—many more times America's total foreign aid budget. (Think Ukraine, Israel, Afghanistan, Iraq, Ethiopia, and more.)[3]

If you're an occasional or moderate drinker, you may arch an eyebrow. "You're making a case about abuse," you're thinking, "when the issue is lack of self-control."

I agree with you. But given genetic predisposition, a first drink can be like gambling with physiology. So, short of testing my genetic luck, my surest safeguard against abuse is nonuse. "*First the man takes a drink*," says an old Japanese proverb. "*Then the drink takes a drink. Then the drink takes the man.*"

The *Lancet* medical journal calls the *Global Burden of Disease* research "the most comprehensive effort to date to understand the changing health challenges around the world." Since 1990 it's formed a mountain of data from two hundred and four countries. Last year, within that research, the Bill & Melinda Gates Foundation's alcohol study drew the attention of *Fortune* magazine. A person's health is at risk, the study said, "at any more than two teaspoons of wine or two and a half tablespoons of beer a day."[4] A year earlier at Oxford University a study of more than 25,000 people similarly found "no safe dose of alcohol" in terms of brain health.[5]

Members of the UK's Independent Scientific Committee on Drugs used sixteen criteria to study twenty top drugs—including heroin, crack cocaine, methamphetamine, tobacco, cannabis, ecstasy, and alcohol—for harm to the user and to others. On a 100-point scale, alcohol came in at 72 points, overall the most harmful drug. Heroin and crack cocaine scored 55 and 54 points, respectively. (Heroin, crack cocaine, and methamphetamine harm individual users most, but their weighted totals placed them well behind alcohol.)

Closer to home, *Forbes* reported that more than half of

the trauma patients in emergency rooms got there because they hurt themselves after drinking.[6] Dr. Harris Stratyner, former director of addiction recovery services at Mount Sinai Medical Center, calls alcohol "a worthless drug that affects every single cell in your body."[7]

———◇◇◇◇◇———

I'm puzzled by America's position on its third-leading cause of preventable death, right after tobacco use and poor diet/exercise. When tobacco dangers grew too obvious to ignore, the U.S. surgeon general issued warnings, governments raised taxes on tobacco products, and legislatures passed laws forbidding sales to minors. Congress held hearings. The media ran public service announcements. Public spaces outlawed smoking. In the U.S. at least, smoking became taboo.

Then, in 1998, fifty-two state and territory attorneys general entered into a Master Settlement Agreement with the four largest tobacco companies in the country to settle dozens of state lawsuits brought to recover billions of dollars in healthcare costs associated with treating smoking-related illnesses. Forty-five tobacco companies eventually settled with the states in a twenty-five-year, $246 billion settlement—the largest civil litigation settlement in U.S. history. Among the positive results, cigarette consumption dropped by more than fifty percent between 1998 and 2019.[8]

In the same crusading spirit, America tackles obesity and its handmaidens—calories, sugar, processed foods, lack of exercise. But our national response to alcohol consists largely of reminding people not to drink and drive.

Tobacco's damage stays mostly with the user. No one careens into oncoming traffic under the influence of nicotine. No one beats his wife after one too many cigarettes or creates an unwanted pregnancy in a night of heavy smoking. And still our national guidelines for alcohol are comparatively muted.

Given alcohol's often destructive march through lives, marriages, families, and businesses, more people are choosing to do without it. In 1986, after an embarrassing dinner conversation the night before, a well-known Texan gave up alcohol. Has it made any difference? In his bestselling memoir, *Decision Points,* George W. Bush writes, "There's no way to know where my life would have headed if I hadn't made the decision to quit drinking, but I am certain I would not be recording these thoughts as a former governor of Texas and president of the United States."[9]

Anne Hathaway is an Academy Award winner and one of the highest-grossing actresses of the twenty-first century. In 2019, shortly after the birth of her first son, she announced a moratorium on alcohol for eighteen years. "I'm going to stop drinking while my son is in my house," she said. "I don't totally love the way I do it and he really does need me all the time in the mornings. The time I have with him is really precious. I hate to say it—as you get older, the hangovers get really bad . . . I had to make a choice and I chose mornings."[10]

Last year, my friend Kristian Stanfill, a marvelously talented Christian musician and songwriter, shared a moving account of his two-year sobriety journey with the ninety thousand people following him on Instagram. "Somebody needs to hear that sobriety isn't just possible but it's also worth it," he wrote. "My life is not perfect and the last 730 days has not been easy but I'm happier and healthier than I ever was with a drink in my hand. My head is clear, and my relationships are real. My heart is ON and I'm dreaming again. I'm checked in to reality and I'm fighting to be present in every moment. This is the good life. Beauty from ashes. Something worth fighting for."[11]

———◦◦◦◦◦◦———

Finally, as in all of life, unrelated to anything we say or preach, and whether or not we ever see it, certain choices we make will have an area of influence, and that matters too. I had finished outlining this book in 2006 when I asked my three children one morning what kinds of decisions should go in a book about life wisdom. Mookie was fourteen at the time and spoke first. "I can tell you one thing," he said, "I think it's wise that you've never had anything to drink." Until that moment, I hadn't planned a chapter on the subject, but the speed of my son's reply struck me.

Chapter 20

ANTICIPATE DEATHBED REGRETS
Take Steps Now to Avoid Regrets

The bitterest tears shed over graves are for
words left unsaid and deeds left undone.
—Harriet Beecher Stowe

Billy Graham preached in person to more people than anyone else in all of history—an estimated two hundred million. Few public figures of the past century hold more respect. In the annual Gallup Poll of "America's Most Admired Men," Mr. Graham appeared in the top ten a record fifty-three times, more than any other man since the list's inception in 1948.

Would it surprise you to know that the man who held the world's ear and counseled every American president from Dwight D. Eisenhower to Barack Obama had regrets? In his autobiography, *Just As I Am*, the renowned evangelist confessed that in taking on the world he lost something important at home:

This is a difficult subject for me to write about, but over the years, the Billy Graham Evangelistic Association and the Team became my second family without my realizing it. Ruth says those of us who were off traveling missed the best part of our lives—enjoying the children as they grew. She is probably right. I was too busy preaching all over the world.

Only Ruth and the children can tell what those extended times of separation meant to them. For myself, as I look back, I now know that I came through those years much the poorer both psychologically and emotionally. I missed so much by not being home to see the children grow and develop.[1]

———◇◇◇———

For decades Nelson Mandela was the iconic leader of the resistance for blacks under the South African race segregation known as apartheid. Led by his sacrifice, an entire nation rallied for liberty. And yet in 1992, not long after he was released from twenty years behind bars on Robben Island, before a horde of reporters in Johannesburg, Mandela spoke of his most profound loss. "It seems to be the destiny of freedom fighters to have unstable personal lives," he said. "When your life is the struggle, as mine was, there is little room left for family. That has always been my greatest regret, and the most painful aspect of the choice I made."[2]

At the wedding of his daughter Zindzi, Mandela agonized afresh: "We watched our children growing without our guidance. When I did come out of prison, my children said, 'We thought we had a father and one day he'd come back. But to our dismay, our father came back, and he left us alone because he has now become the father of the nation.'"

Tormented, in his autobiography Mandela wrote, "To be the father of a nation is a great honor, but to be the father of a family is a greater joy. But it was a joy I had far too little of."[3]

Those of us off the world stage live no less in the shadow of choices made and things undone: prime hours on the road or in the office, marriage to the "wrong" person, fitness and health gone to seed, money gone before the spending ended, children grown before we knew them.

Even in high school, I could see that while a person can live only a day at a time, life one day presents us with the sum of our actions. Of course my father's early death shaped my thoughts here. Because of it, I noticed when someone around me tried to reverse a harmful habit or lifestyle: the open-heart surgery survivor watching cholesterol, the newly divorced father leaving work early for restricted time with his kids. Even as a teenager I believed if a young man could know adults' most common regrets, he might take steps to avoid them.

Don't think I began right away. My father died at the start of my senior year of high school—not a natural point for a kid to embrace preventive health. For the next eight or ten years, other than switching from whole milk to skim, if it looked good on a dish, I ate it. Except for four years of college football, I coasted on nature's gift to youth. Post-college, I took a few extra pounds in stride. Post-marriage, I made room for a few more. By age twenty-eight, the few-here-few-there effect on the scales was thirty pounds over my college place-kicker weight.

The real kicker was my trip to Dr. Kenneth Cooper, father of the aerobics movement, at his famous clinic in Dallas. Dr. Cooper knows something about heart disease. After my body was measured, scanned, and analyzed, I had sufficient incentive to commit to a life of low-fat foods and regular exercise—routines I've largely kept for more than three decades.

———◇◇◇◇◇———

In my early thirties, my efforts to eliminate deathbed regrets expanded to include my family. By now I was heading my own company and traveling more than I wanted, especially given the ages of my children. Thing one was to give up golf for six years—not to practice or play less, but to walk away from it. At age thirty-eight I resolved that by age forty my business travel would be cut in half, and to seal my resolve, I announced it to my wife.

That resolution proved a little tougher. My work was taking me around the world to people and events that in many cases were making history. Client assignments had me to South Africa, Sudan, England, Scotland, Germany, Honduras, Costa Rica, Peru, Australia, New Zealand, the Netherlands, Bosnia, India, and across the U.S. The people impressed by that schedule, however, did not include my wife and children. If my status with Delta Airlines threatened my status at home, I knew what had to give.

In the coming months, as I began to say no to certain clients and new business opportunities, it got easier, and the business survived. Full and frank disclosure: while my travel may not have downsized a full 50 percent, it shrunk dramatically, increasing my ordinary, routine, normal-living time with my wife and children.

You may be thinking that few employees can choose to decline travel assignments, and you'd be right. But too many entrepreneurs and executives who *can* trim their schedules choose not to. I spoke once to an Important Young Man who traveled widely to Important Places but couldn't recall what grade his daughter was in at school.

"Every day I was absent from my family is gone forever," Billy Graham said with regret. "Although much of that travel was necessary, some of it was not."[4]

Something about the American work schedule, if not anti-family, is perilously close to un-family—as if our spouses and children are what we do when professional pursuits wane. And yet a once-in-a-century seizer of opportunities regrets that every day he was absent from his family is gone forever.

We are what we do every day. What defines us is not a single large intention but a hundred thousand choices of every size when we're tired, satisfied, distracted, full of ourselves, threatened, happy, reactionary, sentimental, hurried, bored . . . We're not talking New Year's resolutions, but that every person chooses sooner or later whether or not to live intentionally. Every week, I hear another story of a marriage too early or to the "wrong" person, personal bankruptcy, a destructive affair, blinding stress, tobacco-related lung cancer or emphysema, a child lost to alcohol or drug abuse, obesity complications . . . as many variations as there are people with prime years to waste.

A few weeks after the Georgia Bulldogs won the 2022 NCAA football national championship, Matt Luke, one of the highest-paid offensive line coaches in the country, walked away, at age forty-five, to be a dad to his two sons, both under age fifteen. He defended his move this way: "All the coaches who had kids and they're going to college, you hear from them, 'Wow, that goes fast, and I wish I would have been there more often.' I didn't want to look back and have regrets.

You don't get this time back," Luke told *Sports Illustrated*. "There won't be any regrets."

The ticking clock intimidates us, frightens us, but while time is unforgiving, God is not. What lies behind us is gone, and consequences come, but God is in the business of redeeming the lost years. We can still give Him the time we have.

Chapter 21

AND ANOTHER THING . . .
A Few More Thoughts

A person who won't read has no
advantage over one who can't read.
—Mark Twain

Here are four small principles that have had an outsize impact on my life, and my personal guarantee that the power of each one far exceeds the space I give it.

The People You Meet, the Books You Read

The late Charles "Tremendous" Jones was a business star turned author and speaker who left audiences with maybe five times more energy and optimism than they brought in. He and my father were friends when I met him by chance as I was selling books door-to-door. That afternoon I lingered in his living room too long for any sales call. But those who knew Charles as a knockout salesman will smile to hear that he bought one of everything in my bag.

Of this remarkable man's many evergreen phrases, the one rooted in me is, "You will be the same person in five years as you are today except for the people you meet and the books you read."

Don't speed past that. For a moment mentally review *your* past five years. In one happenstance conversation, Charles Jones marked the rest of my life. A similar encounter awaits the readers of his books. But while you're at it, extend that life-altering principle to any good person or any good book.

Pat Williams had a fifty-six-year management career in the National Basketball Association. He helped bring the NBA to Orlando. The wildly popular after-dinner speaker tells audiences that reading five books in a category makes you an expert on the topic. Whether or not that's certifiably true, getting your nose into five good books puts you far ahead of the person who never opens one.

Warren Buffet says by the time he was eleven years old he'd read every book on the subject of investing in the Omaha Public Library. Eighty years later he's a billionaire a hundred times over.

My parents so believed in conversation and books that they crowded our dinner table with people who had something to say and raised their kids with no television set. My siblings and I are not all heavy readers—personalities play into that—but we all value the stories and knowledge in other people's lives. We know that TV viewing is a judgment call, not a de facto home fixture, and that the soul of a house most often is in its bookshelves.

After Midnight

Once during college, I arranged to spend the night at my older sister's townhouse to stay out on a date past the school's curfew. Sometime after midnight, I eased through my sister's front door and slipped into her guest room, unaware that she'd waited up to hear me safely in. The next morning over late breakfast, she said in passing that what we do after midnight generally does little good and often causes harm.

Years later at a charity golf outing I was paired with the founder of LA Fitness, a popular fitness chain. Between shots I brought up another national brand that operated a twenty-four-hour facility two miles from our home. I asked him about the business value of such clubs staying open around the clock. "Not much good happens after midnight," he said, explaining why they close at ten.

What is it about the wee hours? Besides the obvious sleep loss, something—the fatigue, the anonymity of the dark—slackens our grip on good judgment. We pour another drink, place another bet, click onto a harmful website. In case I haven't said it to my sister, she'll know when she reads this that I wasn't too sleepy that next morning for her comment to sink in. Now as a father and grandfather, I hear it coming out of my mouth too.

"I'm Sorry"

In a preface to one of her books on etiquette, former White House protocol expert Letitia Baldridge describes a glaring blunder that happened on her watch in President Kennedy's White House. For his first-ever media event as president she set up bars in four corners of a large room, also marking the first Sunday that the White House served alcohol—the kind of gaffe newspapers put in headlines, and they all did.

The president was outraged. Early Monday morning, he called Ms. Baldridge to the Oval Office and unloaded on her. Did the champion of good judgment defend herself? Shift the blame? Attack the newspapers? Plead ignorance? Nope. She was wrong and she said so—something along the lines of, "If I could rent a plane and write 'I am so sorry!' in the sky, I would!" And President Kennedy calmed down. What he wanted to hear was that she knew she was wrong and that she was sorry.

In my personal, social, and business orbits, I've seen deep hurts and potential disasters evaporate in the sunlight of those two words, *I'm sorry*. I've also heard the person making the apology add, "if I offended you" and recharge the thunderclouds. An apology is not about the other person's feelings. It's about the speaker's action. The best addendum to "I'm sorry" is "Please forgive me."

Don't Worry

When I learned not to take personal responsibility for things beyond my control, the ship of my emotions entered calm waters. After that, delayed flights, rotten weather, traffic jams, sick employees, and all manner of inconveniences, even *crises*, shrank to manageable size along with my stress level.

Our firm once was owed $140,000 by a former client who might not have paid even if he could. I couldn't control him, but I could see to it that one head stayed cool. Nearly a year into the payment standoff, we proposed to him that he give us our earned fees in client product, which he promptly shipped to us. We sold the product to other organizations at a discount and all but recouped the year-old receivable.

In the heat of our fees and our former client's refusal, I could have pounded the table and shouted, hired an attorney, fired off demand letters. But by now I was getting a grip on Jesus' words regarding worry, namely that if God knows the hairs on my head, if He knows when a penny-a-dozen sparrow hits the ground, in all likelihood this situation was on His radar.

A colleague reminded me once of the time she couldn't get me to match her anger over a client situation. She looked at me and said, "Aren't you worried?" And I had to admit that, no, I wasn't.

"Not even that they may drop us?" she pressed. "Not really," I said. Leaning back in her chair, she said, "Mark, what *does* worry you these days?" And I heard myself say truthfully, "Not much."

Later my colleague observed to me that such calmness set our corporate culture. That makes sense, and I'm grateful for it. Instead of fretting over who might leave us, I tried to expend energy in hiring the right people. If a client left, I cared but I didn't worry. I sure didn't lose sleep. As for the countless small reverses in a given week, I can't claim to have achieved bliss, but I'm aware that flare-ups only have the fuel we give them.

My father-in-law entitled his bestseller *All You Can Do Is All You Can Do—But All You Can Do Is Enough.* Exactly. We can't control the rain; we *can* pull out an umbrella. We can't control another person's harsh word; we *can* return a soft answer.

There's a reason why Reinhold Niebuhr's deeply human plea is called the Serenity Prayer and people worldwide commit it to memory:

> God, grant me the serenity to accept the things I cannot change, the courage to change the things I can, and the wisdom to know the difference.

Chapter 22

The Wisest Decision Anyone Can Make
Answering the "And Then What?" Question

> *What will it profit a man if he gains the*
> *whole world, and loses his own soul?*
> —Mark 8:36 (NKJV)

My father would tell the story of a law school student discussing his plans for the future:

"Son, tell me about your plans after law school."

"I hope to get a job with a good firm and start making some money."

"That sounds fine. And then what?"

"Well, at some point, and hopefully not too late, I want to get married."

"I hope you do, son. And then what?"

"I want to get a nice house and start a family."

"Of course, and then?"

"And then I want to raise my kids in good schools and earn enough to save for a second home."

"Right, right. What then?"

"By then I hope to be making enough money to slow down and take vacations with my wife and children."

"And then?"

"Well, I guess I'd like to see my kids get married and start their own families. I'd like to see them become independent and financially secure."

"Good goals, all. And what then?"

"If I've taken care of myself, I can hope to live long enough to raise my grandchildren. I hear that's even better than having children."

"I hear that, too. Then what?"

"Well, I hope I'll be healthy enough to enjoy my later years, maybe travel some with my wife and see the world. I want to make the most of retirement and pass along my money to my children so they can benefit as I have."

"And then?"

The young man paused. "I guess then I'll die."

"Yes, you will. And *then* what?"

The thing about this story is that it chronicles the standard-issue American Dream. Who doesn't identify with some or most of this young man's life path? Maybe you've long since completed college, married happily, are well into your career, and just bought a vacation home. Maybe you're blessed with grandchildren and an investment portfolio Charles Schwab would admire. But somewhere on the march of time, every one of us will face the final "and then what?"

What will your answer be?

Answers commonly go something like this: "Well, I hope I'll go to heaven. I'm workin' on it." Or, "I'm not sure, but I'm trying to make it 'up there.'" Or, "I'm just prayin' the Man Upstairs lets me in." Some people admit they have no idea what comes next. Most say they at least hope to go to heaven when they die.

This book is about wisdom. Wouldn't it be wise to take steps now so that when you come to the end of the dream, you *know* what comes next? The wisest decision anyone can make, ever, is to seal his or her eternal destiny: time forever with the One who created you, me, the earth, the solar system, and everything that exists. The decision is whether or not to hand over your life to God, through His Son, Jesus Christ; the alternative is to bank everything on yourself.

One thing about the ol' American Dream is that the fulfillment-and-peace clause is a guaranteed letdown. Even the most impressive businesses can implode overnight, sinking millions in stock portfolios and trusting investors. Children turn up with minds of their own and can break your heart. Dream houses can burn to charcoal. Family members suffer cancer and waste away before our eyes.

At the ripe age of thirty-two, Comedian Dave Chappelle had a $50 million deal with the Comedy Central channel, impressive by every standard of entertainment deals. The ink on the contract was still wet when Chappelle disappeared, only to be spotted eight thousand miles away, in South Africa. He had run away from the *Chappelle Show's* entire third season. Later he confessed, "The higher up I go, for some reason, the less happy I am."

I'm supposing the financial figures in your life are smaller than Dave's, but the consequences of putting money over soul match his zero for zero. If a person could buy happiness or peace, this young comedian would have been at the front of the line.

Twenty years ago Nicole Kidman became the first Australian to win an Academy Award for best actress. In 2019 *Forbes* ranked her as the fourth-highest-paid actress in the world with an annual income of $34 million. She told *Harper's Bazaar Australia*, "Winning an Oscar can show you the emptiness of your own life, which is kind of what it showed me."

Jack Higgins is one of the most successful novelists on earth. More than two hundred fifty million copies of his thrillers have sold in fifty-five languages. When a magazine interviewer asked him what he knew now that he wished he had known earlier in life, he said, "I wish I had known when you get to the top, there is nothing there." I hope he found something else before he died last year at 92.

So, how does a person gain peace right here, right now? Can there be any certainty about God or where we go after death? I'm not talking about joining a church, getting baptized or confirmed, obeying the Ten Commandments, or living a good life. What I'm leading to is a real relationship with the God who made you and loves you unconditionally.

About three hundred and fifty years ago, an influential French mathematician, physicist, and philosopher named Blaise Pascal wrote of a "God-shaped vacuum in the heart of every man which cannot be filled by any created thing, but only by God, the Creator."

"Let us weigh the gain and loss in wagering that God is," Pascal wrote. "Let us consider the two possibilities. If you gain, you gain all; if you lose, you lose nothing. Hesitate not, then, to wager that He is."[1] C.S. Lewis framed it this way: "Aim at heaven and you will get earth thrown in. Aim at earth and you get neither."[2]

Even people unfamiliar with the Bible likely know John 3:16: "For God so loved the world that he gave his one and only Son, that whoever believes in him shall not perish but have eternal life" (NIV). That sums it up. The Source of your life loves you with such extravagance that He sent His Son to pay the price for your sins—"sin" meaning anything that falls short of God's perfection—so that anyone who believes in Him will have eternal life.

What could be wiser than admitting your life is not a self-made proposition? What could be wiser than making this eternal choice sooner than later? I chose God's offer more than fifty years ago. If you still have breath, you can do it now. You can have a personal relationship for the asking.

I can't imagine life without Christ at the center of it. I love Him more than anything, and I want others to know Him as I do. I'm grateful to be able to know that I will go to heaven when I die. You can know it. The Bible makes it clear that we cannot earn our way to heaven; eternal life is not a reward for anything we can do; it's a free gift. As with any gift, we have to accept it to make it ours.

Hundreds of millions of people across this globe can affirm the wisdom of this decision. Almost every one of them would tell you they wish they had made it sooner. If you haven't made it, you can today. Choosing God is as close as a prayer something like this:

> *Dear God, I know I have sinned and cannot save myself. I acknowledge my need for You in my life for eternity and for right now. Today, Lord Jesus, I repent of my sins and invite You to come into my heart and forgive me. Thank You for Your wonderful gift of eternal life, for hearing and answering my prayer, and for coming into my heart and life as You promise You will. Amen.*

If you prayed that prayer and meant it, you just made the wisest decision possible. *Congratulations.* As you come to know God, every person you know, Christians included, will let you down. But God will not, and He will never leave you.

A good thing to do now is to tell someone about your

decision. I'll never forget when our little Madison prayed a similar prayer. Right after, she said, "Let's call the cousins and tell them what I did." One of the greatest joys of my life has been seeing Madison, Mookie, and Georgia mature in their relationships with God—as real in their young lives as in mine.

Next I encourage you to read the Bible every day to grow in your new relationship. Get a translation you can understand easily. You might start in the New Testament book of John for a clear account of the life of Jesus and His message. God speaks to us through the Bible; we can speak to Him in prayer every day, anytime, anywhere.

Finally, I encourage you to find other followers of Christ and spend time with them. Tell them of your decision. Find a place where you can spend time with fellow believers, worship God, and learn and grow in your relationship with Him.

I close with the words of author Max Lucado:

> You can afford many wrong choices in life. You can choose the wrong career and survive, the wrong city and survive, the wrong house and survive. But there is one choice that must be made correctly, and that is your eternal destiny.[3]

If today you made that choice—the wisest decision you could ever make—I'd be honored to hear about it. Write to me at mark@demoss.com.

Chapter 23

Practicing Gratitude
"Happiness Doubled by Wonder"

Gratitude is not only the greatest of
virtues, but the parent of all others.
—Marcus Tullius Cicero

I was in a shopping center picking up a sushi order for our houseguests when April called. Just leave the food for our guests, she said. Go straight to Scottish Rite Hospital. Rett and Foster had been attacked by two Rottweilers and were in serious condition. Our grandsons, six and eight at the time, were riding their bikes in their quiet neighborhood as they had hundreds of other days, when two dogs they didn't know existed chased them, locked their jaws in the boys' small frames, and dragged them about like rag dolls.

I arrived at the hospital to find Rett and Foster lying side by side on gurneys, sedated, wrapped in blood-soaked bandages. We prayed over them before they were wheeled into surgery for doctors to assess the damage and stitch their little bodies back together. Foster was in surgery for three hours, Rett for nearly five. They emerged with hundreds of stitches and the varied repair work of skilled trauma surgeons, plastic surgeons, and other specialists. Internally, the images could terrorize their memories for years or a lifetime.

The hours following April's call to me brought a torrent of emotions. Anger. "Why would anyone own Rottweilers in a suburban neighborhood full of children?" Rage. "If I see those dogs, I'll shoot them on the spot!" Anxiety. "What if our boys have permanent muscle or neurological damage?" A cry for justice: "This dog owner will pay! Where are the laws?"

In May 2021 the pandemic limited how many people could stay overnight with patients. April remained at the hospital with our daughter and son-in-law and Rett and Foster. I went home with plans to return in the morning. That night as I tried to sleep, still reeling from the turmoil and horror of the day, one emotion profoundly overtook all others: *gratitude*.

The more I learned about dog attacks in general, and about the attacks on our precious boys, the more gratitude welled inside me. Many children die from such maulings, but Rett and Foster were alive. A neighbor named Mary Ellen sustained wounds on her own body while freeing Foster from the dog's iron grip long enough for him to go for his mother. Then God sent a second angel to that cul-de-sac. Hearing the boys' screams, a swimming pool contractor named Joey swung into action. Joey also is an ex-marine. He was finishing a pool installation next door to the house where the dogs lived. With military instincts and brute strength he charged into the mayhem, extracted Rett's neck from the second Rottweiler's jaw, and protected our boy until professional first responders arrived. More gratitude. Overwhelming gratitude.

How grateful I am that Rett and Foster's little brother, George, chose to stay behind with his mother that evening. His four-year-old body most certainly would not have survived the killer clenches and frenzy of dogs weighing a hundred pounds-plus.

Did I say I *felt* gratitude? At times it comes with emotion, but to be clear, gratitude is a response to God's sovereignty and providence, both of which I've experienced in full measure. For the times I've wished for more sovereignty than providence, a Montana pastor named Levi Lusko observes that, "In His providence God can redeem what in His sovereignty He could have prevented." True, God didn't prevent this dog attack, but He continues to redeem it. I'm grateful that He is God, and I am not. The gold thread of gratitude weaves inextricably through my sixty years on this earth.

———◇◇◇◇———

As I write, I remain in remission from the lymphoma diagnosed six years ago. When I was ten years old, my mother recovered from brain surgery to remove a malignant tumor.

As the latest revision of this book comes off the presses, she turns eighty-five. I'm grateful to God who healed a mother and son of cancer some fifty years apart.

"I'm glad God saved your grandsons and healed you and your mother," some of my readers are thinking, "but that's not my story. My loved one *died* of cancer, and we live every day with the heartache and pain." (While our little boys were still recovering from their dog attack, a young mother and father in a neighboring state were grieving the death of their five-month-old son and two-year-old daughter following an unthinkable attack by their own pit bulls.)

I understand that my story isn't everyone's story, but gratitude can be. My story isn't all healing and victory either. I was seventeen when my father died, leaving my forty-year-old mother widowed with seven children. "You're grateful for that, Mark?" Yes, grateful that God has been a "defender of the widow and a father to the fatherless" these more than forty years.

———◇◇◇◇◇———

Seven years after my father died, my brother was killed in a head-on car collision. Where's the gratitude in that? Jesus is a friend who "sticks closer than a brother," and I am grateful. Even in the death of my father and brother, the loss of my childhood home to fire, the cancer and untold other hurts and pain, I embrace these words of Dietrich Bonhoeffer, "In ordinary life, we hardly realize that we receive a great deal more than we give, and that it is only with gratitude that life becomes rich."[1]

It is only with gratitude that a life becomes rich. Why a chapter on gratitude in a book about wisdom? Because wisdom recognizes a Higher order. Because wisdom acknowledges that the primary object of gratitude is outside of ourselves. Because gratitude takes nothing for granted, which is wisdom itself. On the flip side, people lacking gratitude generally have a sense of entitlement—as if they're somehow owed good health, a steady income, a smooth road. Lack of gratitude breeds selfishness; when things fail to go as expected, it opens a door to bitterness.

———◆◇◆———

Ingratitude is hardly new. When Jesus walked on this earth, He came across ten lepers one day who pleaded for mercy, for God's healing touch. He gave them simple instructions to present themselves to the priest, and all ten were healed. The New Testament records that only one of the former lepers returned to glorify God and thank Him. "Were there not ten cleansed?" Jesus asked. "But where are the nine?"

In the Old Testament, the small book of Lamentations records the afflictions of the nation of Israel and the response of the prophet Jeremiah. "The steadfast love of the Lord never ceases," Jeremiah wrote. "His mercies never come to an end; they are new every morning" (Lamentations 3:22–23 ESV). Notice that the prophet doesn't say the Lord's mercies are *renewed* each morning, though that would be amazing. He says God's mercies are *new* every morning, in spite of—maybe along with—loss and illness and struggle and death. I celebrate more than twenty-two thousand mornings of new mercies from the God of heaven. How could I not overflow with gratitude?

A thank-you is an action. Gratitude is a posture, a way of life. The nine lepers notwithstanding, it's easy to be grateful when we're happy and healthy; a wise person also finds gratitude in the valleys. During my battle with cancer, a verse in Psalms appeared to me in a new light: "When my anxious thoughts multiply within me, Your comfort delights my soul" (Psalm 94:19 NASB). Focusing on God's comfort rather than my circumstances lifted me to a life-giving spirit of gratitude, making me happier and more complete—and much less anxious.

———◦◦◦◦◦———

Not that we need academic confirmation, but research supports and underscores the tangible effects of gratitude. Harvard Medical School reports on the research of

Dr. Robert Emmons of the University of California, Davis, and Dr. Michael McCullough of the University of Miami. In one study, the psychologists directed participants to keep a weekly record. One group recorded what they were grateful for. A second group noted what displeased them. The third recorded what events affected them. After ten weeks, the people who made time to record their gratitude were more optimistic and felt better about their lives. Interestingly, they also exercised more and had fewer visits to physicians than the study participants who recorded their aggravations. From his place as the leader of the science of gratitude, Professor Emmons says with some authority that it "reduces lifetime risk for depression, anxiety and substance abuse disorders, and is a key resiliency factor in prevention of suicide."[2]

English philosopher and Christian apologist G. K. Chesterton was marked by gratitude. He became a Christian and joined the church out of gratitude. "I would maintain that thanks are the highest form of thought," he wrote once, "and that gratitude is happiness doubled by wonder."[3]

Six centuries before Chesterton, German theologian and philosopher Meister Eckhart summed up gratitude in one short truth: "If the only prayer you said was thank you, that would be enough."[4] Amen.

Chapter 24

FINISHING WELL
Living Well Until You're Finished Living

> *I have fought the good fight, I have*
> *finished the race, I have kept the faith.*
> —2 Timothy 4:7 (NIV)

On my phone I keep a list of names that records an ugly side of my career. I keep it because it strengthens my resolve to finish well. For these are names of leaders who didn't finish well—not random names, but people I know, or knew, and worked with closely. Most were pastors. Some led large ministries. Collectively they presided over organizations with annual budgets exceeding two *billion* dollars a year, affecting souls by the millions.

This chapter didn't appear in the first edition of this *Little Red Book*, probably because at age forty-five, when I wrote it, I presumed my finish line was still out of sight. Also, at the time I'd personally witnessed only one big public fall. In this return to writing about the journey of wisdom, it struck me that how we finish has less to do with how we start and everything to do with how we walk, which is the point of wisdom.

———◦◦◇◦◦———

To think of finishing well as the final laps of a sixty-, seventy-, or eighty-year run can be daunting if not demoralizing. Who has that kind of staying power and discipline? That's why I define finishing well as *living well until you're finished living*. Given that few are privy to the date and time of our finish, to my thinking this is the only meaningful definition. My father's finish came at age fifty-three, catching us all by surprise, as did my younger brother's death a few years later when he was twenty-two. I'm sixty-one years old now and my desire to cross the line with my integrity intact is almost an obsession, intensified by my recent rediscovery of fifteen words.

For roughly half of my life, I've read through the New Testament three times a year. Then one day last year, for the first time in some ninety readings, a verse in John's gospel grabbed me by the neck and shook me: *"From that time many of His disciples went back and walked with Him no more"* (John 6:66 NKJV, emphasis added). "The sixth chapter of John's Gospel . . . begins with five thousand men following Jesus," pastor and theologian John Piper writes. "And it ends with eleven."[1]

How is it possible? The men and women who quit on

Jesus had *walked* with Him. Heard Him teach. Witnessed His miracles. Just the day before He'd fed five thousand. When they left Him, they didn't just walk away; they rejected His teaching. In the next verse, Jesus turned to the twelve still with Him and said, *"Do you also want to go away?"* Even in that group one would soon betray Him to His executioners.

I offer this look at finishing well not with self-righteous judgment, I hope, but with healthy fear from years of sobering observation. My work brought me to the crash scenes of high-level leaders who veered off course in their personal lives, their marriages, their families, their professions. Public service became public disasters. Private lives became public spectacles. The sweep of the collateral damage is impossible to measure.

Half of the disasters were in churches among the largest in the U.S. Many of the casualties were men I had admired. Now here I was helping them navigate ridicule and gossip from the buzz in the next office to explosive headlines around the world. Hurt and rage gushed from televised church meetings and hemorrhaged across social media. Friends were stunned, families devastated, staff members disillusioned and angry. Reporters were gleeful. While believers everywhere staggered from the blow to Christianity and often to their own faith, the secular world sneered and called it hypocrisy. Again.

God alone can see into men's hearts, but I saw enough to begin to recognize at least the top-line warning signs of a leader's fall, starting with a sense of invincibility, as if rules are for other people. The more successful the leader, the more entrenched the delusion.

"And all who were slain by her were strong men" (7:26 NKJV) says Proverbs, nailing the truism that in our strengths lie the seeds of our weaknesses. Every person on the list in my phone declined to station guardrails at the usual sinkholes and cliffs. This book broaches hazards like alcohol and time alone with a non-spouse member of the opposite sex. In those two areas alone, thoughtful boundaries would have forestalled disaster for at least seventy percent of the men on my list.

In my experience the long-distance runners most likely to stumble are invariably master rationalizers, leaders who generally reject meaningful authority and accountability. Seldom do their inner circles include a devil's advocate, someone free to challenge, push back, spur a second look at an action or decision—let alone to say no. In most cases, by the time I'm involved, once-honorable men have lost the common sense and good instincts to avoid even the appearance of impropriety.

Pride, arrogance, entitlement, bad judgment, ignorance of the court of public opinion—these are common denominators in most falls from grace. I've seen too many leaders want their successes on the evening news and their personal lives out of everyone else's purview, which is wishful thinking. Leaders are first of all servants, not kings to be served. The ones who lose sight of the source of their support, the font of their funding, the lives of their constituents, become weak and vulnerable.

Certainly there are cases when a diminished leader arguably did not sin, but a day comes when that point is no longer the point. What's not up for argument—what's irrefutable—is that in every case, the leader in question showed poor judgment, a lack of wisdom. One doesn't have to be guilty of sin to do something stupid.

———◇◇◇◇———

Even too much of a "right" thing, like pouring your life into serving others, can be deadly. A man I know of, not on my list, gained renown for founding two of the largest humanitarian organizations in the world. In the process he also lost his family. "He traveled ten months of the year, which made it difficult," his daughter wrote in his biography. "My parents' marriage suffered, my father's health was broken, my sister and I barely knew our father."

This absentee father recited a credo that must have cut his children to the core. "I've made an agreement with God," he would say. "I'll take care of his helpless little lambs overseas if He'll take care of mine at home."

The longer he stayed away, the less there was to go home to. "In 1963 he had a nervous breakdown," a magazine reported.

"For nine months he almost disappeared, preferring to travel the world rather than return home. In 1967 he resigned from [the first organization he founded], bitter at those he felt interfered with his ministry. On a 1968 good-bye tour of Asia, one daughter reached him by phone to ask if he could come home. He refused, saying he wanted to extend his trip to Vietnam. His wife started home immediately, but by the time she arrived, [the daughter] had tried to commit suicide. Later that year, she tried again and succeeded. By then her father was hospitalized in Switzerland where he would stay for a year."

In 1970, this global Christian figure legally separated from his wife. In 1978, his family met with him to try to reconcile. Four days later he was dead. A quarter century after that a writer referred to him as "an imperfect instrument," which of course describes every one of us. God uses broken vessels—which I say with abject gratitude—but a person ignorant of his or her brokenness is of little use to anyone.

This chapter is not about perfection. It's about maturing in God's grace, about moving forward *daily* in our humanness, and in His holiness, in the race set before us. As C. S. Lewis said, "If you are on the wrong road, progress means doing an about-turn and walking back to the right road; and in that case, the man who turns back soonest is the most progressive man."[2]

I'm preaching to myself as much as to anyone. We all come to moments with our names on them, situations uncannily crafted to catch the toe of a shoe and send us flying. As we grow in wisdom, as we more quickly recognize our foibles and blind spots and learn to plan against them, maybe, increasingly, we can avoid some of what stands to hurt us and others. As a friend of mine would say with a smile, "It's constant vigilance." *We are human.*

But we are humans with choices. When news of another leader's fall reverberates through the mediasphere, a common reaction is to resist judging. "There but for the grace of God go I," someone will say, and it's true, again, that we all are prone to sin. The words "but for the grace of God" suggest, however, that we are somehow helpless, which we are not. We have agency. In our marathon runs, God's grace is essential and life-giving, but I largely determine what affects my pace and distance. To rely solely on God to protect me from myself is to discharge all personal responsibility for my outcomes.

If you heard that a drunk driver sped a hundred miles an hour down the wrong side of the road at 2:30 A.M., and killed five people in an oncoming van, you wouldn't say, "There but for the grace of God go I." The driver chose to drink. He chose to stay out into the wee hours when thinking blurs and defenses dip. Before the first drink, he chose whether or not to hand off his car keys. To a great degree, a person chooses when and whether to test God's grace.

———◦◇◦———

Another common response, usually as a vote to forgive and restore (or to excuse) a fallen leader, is to bring up the king in the Bible who slept with a military officer's wife and then sent him to the front lines for certain death. "Look at David," someone will say, "he was 'a man after God's own heart.'"

To be clear, David was not after God's heart the day he had Bathsheba brought to his room. That description was used forty-five years earlier when David was twelve years old and marked by God as a future king of Israel. "The LORD has sought for Himself a man after His own heart," the prophet Samuel said to King Saul. (1 Samuel 13:14 NKJV).

The rest of the story is that God sent the prophet Nathan to David with a fourfold list of severe consequences for his sin. The sword would never depart from his house; the Lord would raise up adversaries within David's own house; his wives would be given to his neighbors to lie with in the open sun. That's three. When David finally confessed to Nathan, the prophet assured him the Lord had put away his sin and he would not die. "However," Nathan added, "because by this deed you have given great occasion to the enemies of the LORD to blaspheme, the child also who is born to you shall surely die" (2 Samuel 12:14 NKJV).

As with David, wounded leaders can and often do resume productive work and ministry, but always at a cost, and seldom at the previous level. Of the names on my list, none has returned to his former influence. Some are out of ministry altogether.

———◆◇◆◇◆———

No one finishes well by accident, of that I'm certain. I carry a far longer list (this one in my heart) of men and women who have finished the race or continue to inspire me by their running with integrity.

What qualities do they share? Invariably, they're marked by humility. The world revolves but not around them. They know their influence and accept the responsibility that comes with it.

They factor in their fallibilities, countering their human natures with spiritual disciplines like regular prayer and Scripture reading. Proverbs is the gold standard for preventive wisdom. I can't say that reading God's Word daily guarantees you will finish well, but I can promise you that *not* doing it increases the odds that you *won't*.

On my mental list of endurance runners no one is perfect, but to a person they know the value of prudence; they work at being discreet, circumspect. To a person, they routinely apply the "Wisdom Test" to appraise a situation not just by asking "Is it legal, moral, or ethical?" but "Is it wise?" More than just accept accountability and authority, they actively seek them out.

The men and women I know who are living well or have finished well are people with guardrails. I could chart the correlation between wisdom and guardrails in one's life. A leader wanting to beat the system will find a way, but for simple prudence even small precautions deflect a range of potential troubles. One of the most successful leaders I know—*the* leader in his field by one standard of measurement—once let me in on some of the protective measures that mark his daily life.

To start, he has the passwords to none of his devices and apps. His internet has a filter. (A Google search for "hot air balloons," for example, would be blocked based on the first word.) Other programs keep his staff apprised in real time of where he is and his every credit card purchase. We all have days we'd like to detour from the race into "just this once," but my friend also wants to live well until he's finished living. Before God and others, he knows not to leave that to chance.

Heeding the prophet Nathan about giving occasion to the enemies of the Lord, strong finishers maintain a healthy fear of *not* finishing well—of handing out the ammunition to get shot at.

———◈———

The key to finishing well, I'm convinced, is *today*. Forever is too long, too much. Tomorrow holds no guarantees. I can't presume that I'll live well until the end, but I can live well today. I can't be faithful to my wife forever if I'm not faithful to her today. I can't swear to sobriety for all my days, but I can decline to drink this day. I can't assume I'll always be the father I should be, but I'm sure I can love my children well today. Can I master my tongue or take in God's Word forever? Who knows. But I can guard my tongue today; I can read the Bible today. All we have, ever, is today.

The Old Testament prophet Micah gives straightforward directions to the finish line. "And what does the Lord require of you," he writes, "but to do justly, to love mercy, and to walk humbly with your God?" (Micah 6:8 nkjv). We can try doing that today.

This brings me back to my father's example in my early life. If finishing well means living well until we're finished living, then may the prayer of Moses—"The man of God"—that was found on my dad's nightstand the day he died, stay engraved on my heart:

> So teach us to number our days,
> That we may present to You a heart of
> wisdom.
>
> —Psalm 90:12 (nasb)

Selah.

Now unto the King eternal, immortal, invisible, the only wise God, be honour and glory forever and ever. Amen.

—1 Timothy 1:17 (KJV)

Acknowledgments

Writing a book doesn't happen without help. Thank you, HarperCollins Christian Publishing, for believing in me and in this subject enough to invest your name and resources three times over. This is the second revision of my original book, and I'm grateful for everyone who brought my thoughts and words to the printed page.

I'm grateful for those who bought this book, enough of you to warrant rereleasing it twice. Some of you thought enough of it to order more copies to share with others, like the school principal who passed out one hundred twenty-five copies to his graduating class, the parents who placed books on the forty-five seats at their child's wedding rehearsal dinner, the radio executive who distributed copies to his two hundred employees, the college president who gave five hundred books to the faculty and staff at the beginning of the academic year, the political advisor who was the first to order one hundred books, the U.S. congressman who asked for sixty to give to newly elected officials across his state, the national retail chain founder who sent copies to his five hundred store managers, and to all of you who simply read *The Little Red Book* and shared it with a sibling, parent, child, or friend.

Thank you, Robert Wolgemuth, for showing me how to convert an idea and a vision to a book that is actually publishable. Nancy Lovell shares my love for words—she's just better at stringing them together, replacing a good word with a better one, or removing extra words. Your touch improved every paragraph. Thank you.

Over the course of my career at DeMoss, some one hundred colleagues carried my name on their business cards, something I never took lightly. Thank you all for joining our cause, and for making me better and wiser.

I benefited also from incredible opportunities and experiences from our clients over the twenty-eight-year life of our PR firm. Thank you for your confidence and trust in me and my team—I take neither for granted.

The late Jerry Falwell Sr. invested in me as a young college graduate, crowding his lifetime of experiences into our eight years together. He was a better friend than I deserved. My wisdom journey has been enriched by many pastor friends who have taught and modeled wise living. I'm forever in their debt.

I'm blessed with the greatest in-laws anyone could ask or pray for. Thank you, Art and Angela, for your daughter, your love, and your enthusiasm for this book.

On several pages, I write about my late father. Though he died in 1979, he remains the wisest person in my life. We shared only seventeen years on this earth, but I owe him much, and he was an impetus for this book. Thank you, Dad, for modeling a heart and a life of wisdom.

My mother is the remarkable woman who woke up one September morning in 1979 as a forty-year-old widow with seven children, one of whom would die seven years later. Not until I was married with children of my own would I appreciate the difference between losing a spouse and a son, and losing a parent and a sibling. Thank you, Mother, for your steady strength. Thank you for loving me through every stage.

Seeing wisdom in the lives of my children, their spouses, and now their children is more gratifying than I can adequately express.

Thank you, April . . . for everything. I adore you.

Above all, thank you, Lord, for picking me up and placing me where you have, like a turtle on a fencepost.

Notes

FOREWORD

1. Winston Churchill, *My Early Life: 1874–1904* (London: T. Butterworth; New York: Scribner, 1930).

CHAPTER 1: STAY UNDER THE UMBRELLA

1. "Number of Jobs, Labor Market Experience, Marital Status, and Health: Results from a National Longitudinal Survey Summary," U.S. Bureau of Labor Statistics, August 31, 2021, https://www.bls.gov/news.release/nlsoy .nr0.htm.
2. Mission, The Salvation Army International, https://salvationarmy.org/ihq /Mission.
3. Robert A. Watson with Ben Brown, *The Most Effective Organization in the U.S.: Leadership Secrets of the Salvation Army* (New York: Crown Business, 2001).

CHAPTER 4: WORK LESS, THINK MORE

1. Joey Reiman, *Thinking for a Living: Creating Ideas that Revitalize your Business, Career, and Life* (Atlanta: Longstreet, 2001).
2. Albert Einstein quote, Goodreads, https://www.goodreads.com/quotes /320600-we-can-not-solve-our-problems-with-the-same-level.
3. Chris Kolmar, "53 Stunning Social Media Statistics," Zippia, September 29, 2022, https://www.zippia.com/advice/social-media-statistics/.
4. Adam Smith, *Supermoney* (Hoboken, New Jersey: John Wiley & Sons, 1972), 180.
5. Joey Reiman, *Thinking for a Living*.
6. "Is This Man the Next Billy Graham?" *TIME* magazine, September 17, 2001, https://content.time.com/time/magazine/0,9263,7601010917,00.html.

CHAPTER 5: TECHNOLOGY ISN'T EVERYTHING

1. "Gartner Says Only 9% of Customers Report Solving Their Issues Completely via Self-Service," Gartner, September 25, 2019, https://www.gartner.com/en

/newsroom/press-releases/2019–09–25-gartner-says-only-9—of-customers
-report-solving-thei.

2. Julian Borger, "Tired of Talking to a Machine? Find a Human with a Cheat Sheet," *The Guardian*, November 24, 2005, https://www.theguardian.com /world/2005/nov/25/usa.julianborger.

3. William James, *Forbes* Quotes, https://www.forbes.com/quotes/10031/.

4. "Teens, Social Media and Technology 2022," Pew Research Center, August 10, 2022, https://www.pewresearch.org/internet/2022/08/10 /teens-social-media-and-technology-2022/.

5. Glenn Gamboa, "John Mayer Won't Tweet, Don't Ask," *Newsday*, October 14, 2010, https://www.newsday.com/beta/news/john-mayer-won-t-tweet-don-t -ask-a84165.

6. Henri Nouwen, *New Oxford Review* (June 1987), in "Classic & Contemporary Excerpts from August 12, 1988," *Christianity Today*, https://www .christianitytoday.com/ct/1988/august-12/reflections.html.

7. Eric Schmidt, "The Courage to be Unreasonable," Penn Commencement 2009, *UPenn Almanac* Vol. 55 No. 34, May 26, 2009, https://almanac.upenn .edu/archive/volumes/v55/n34/comm-schmidt.html.

Chapter 6: Buy Some Stamps

1. James Fallows, "Why the Internet Isn't the Death of the Post Office," *The New York Times*, September 4, 2005, https://www.nytimes.com/2005/09/04 /technology/why-the-internet-isnt-the-death-of-the-post-office.html.

2. Lisa Grunwald and Stephen J. Adler, *Letters of the Century: 1900–1999* (New York: Dial Press, 2008).

3. James Fallows, "Why the Internet Isn't the Death of the Post Office."

4. Phil Mickelson, *One Magical Sunday: (But Winning Isn't Everything)* (New York: Grand Central, 2007).

5. Rick Reilly, "Wooden Set the Bar High," ESPN, June 7, 2010, https://www .espn.com/espn/news/story?id=5260677.

Chapter 8: Money Isn't Everything; Good People Are

1. "Global Engagement and Wellbeing Remain Stable, But Not Great," *State of the Global Workplace: 2022 Report*, Gallup, https://www.gallup.com /workplace/349484/state-of-the-global-workplace.aspx#ite-393245.

Chapter 10: And Another Thing . . .

1. Milan Kundera quote, Goodreads, https://www.goodreads.com /quotes/8485582-in-any-case-it-seems-to-me-that-all-over.

Chapter 12: The Wisdom of Firsts

1. Charles H. Spurgeon, Psalm 119:147, *The Treasury of David* (London: Passmore and Alabaster, 1884–86).

2. Bill Gates, *TIME* magazine, January 13, 1997.

3. Recounted in John Ortberg, *The Life You've Always Wanted* (Grand Rapids, Michigan: Zondervan, 2015).

4. Ron Chernow, *Titan: The Life of John D. Rockefeller Sr.* (New York: Vintage Books, 2004).

5. George Jenkins, "Lessons from Our Founder: Give Back," Publix, https://corporate.publix.com/about-publix/culture/lessons-from-our-founder.

CHAPTER 13: A TURTLE ON A FENCEPOST

1. Allan C. Emery, *A Turtle on a Fencepost: Little Lessons of Large Importance* (Houston, Texas: World Wide Publishing, 1980).

2. Tiger Woods, *How I Play Golf* (New York: Grand Central, 2001).

3. Antonya English, "Spurrier Still Has Soft Spot for Duke," *Tampa Bay Times*, August 10, 2001, https://www.tampabay.com/archive/2001/08/10/spurrier-still-has-soft-spot-for-duke/.

4. "Fred Rogers Acceptance Speech–1997," The Emmy Awards, YouTube, https://www.youtube.com/watch?v=Upm9LnuCBUM.

CHAPTER 14: THERE ARE NO DEGREES OF INTEGRITY

1. "Ernst & Young to Pay $100 Million Penalty for Employees Cheating on CPA Ethics Exams and Misleading Investigation," U.S. Securities and Exchange Commission, June 28, 2022, https://www.sec.gov/news/press-release/2022-114.

2. Tovia Smith and Jaclyn Diaz, "Rick Singer, Head of the College Admissions Bribery Scandal, Gets 42 Months in Prison," NPR, January 4, 2023, https://www.npr.org/2023/01/04/1146837418/rick-singer-sentenced-varsity-blues-college-admissions-bribery-scandal.

3. "National Leadership Index 2005: A National Study of Confidence in Leadership," Center for Public Leadership, John F. Kennedy School of Government, Harvard University.

4. Karl Eller, *Integrity is All You've Got* (New York: McGraw-Hill, 2004).

5. Karl Eller, *Integrity is All You've Got*.

6. Jon M. Huntsman Sr., *Barefoot to Billionaire: Reflections on a Life's Work and a Promise to Cure Cancer* (New York: Harry N. Abrams, 2015).

7. Jon M. Huntsman, *Barefoot to Billionaire*.

CHAPTER 16: THE WISDOM OF AGE

1. "Lehman: Meeting Wooden 'One of the Highlights of My Life'," *Golf Digest*, June 5, 2010, https://www.golfdigest.com/story/lehman-meeting-wooden-one-of-the-highlights-of-my-life.

2. "Coach John Wooden makes Bill Walton get a haircut," 805Bruin, YouTube, https://www.youtube.com/watch?v=4OPu3fnbmvo&t=136s.

CHAPTER 19: HERE'S TO NOT DRINKING AT ALL

1. *Golf World* [now *Golf Digest*], September 1998, in "John Daly is Drinking Again," CBS News, September 21, 1998, https://www.cbsnews.com/news /john-daly-is-drinking-again/.

2. "Alcohol Facts and Statistics," National Institute on Alcohol Abuse and Alcoholism, updated March 2022, https://www.niaaa.nih.gov/publications /brochures-and-fact-sheets/alcohol-facts-and-statistics.

3. "Alcohol Facts and Statistics," National Institute on Alcohol Abuse and Alcoholism.

4. Chloe Taylor, "Bombshell Alcohol Study Funded by Bill & Melinda Gates Foundation Finds Only Risks, Zero Benefits for Young Adults," *Fortune*, July 15, 2022, https://fortune.com/2022/07/15/alcohol-study-lancet-young -adults-should-not-drink-bill-melinda-gates-foundation/.

5. Natalie Grover, "Any Amount of Alcohol Consumption Harmful to the Brain, Finds Study," *The Guardian*, May 18, 2021, https://www.theguardian .com/society/2021/may/18/any-amount-of-alcohol-consumption-harmful -to-the-brain-finds-study.

6. Liz Moyer, "Reinventing Rehab," *Forbes*, April 19, 2006, https://www.forbes .com/2006/04/15/addiction-rehab-reinvention_cx_lm_06slate_0418rehab .html.

7. Matthew Herper, "Cutting Alcohol's Cost," *Forbes*, August 22, 2006, www .forbes.com/2006/08/22/health-drinking-problems_cx_mh_nightlife06 _0822costs.html.

8. "The Master Settlement Agreement," National Association of Attorneys General, https://www.naag.org/our-work/naag-center-for-tobacco -and-public-health/the-master-settlement-agreement/.

9. George W. Bush, *Decision Points* (New York: Crown, 2011).

10. Anne Hathaway interview, *The Ellen Degeneres Show*, January 19, 2019, in Hannah Yasharoff, "Anne Hathaway Reveals She's Giving Up Drinking for the Next 18 Years," *USA Today*, January 19, 2019, https://www.usatoday.com /story/life/entertainthis/2019/01/22/anne-hathaway-quitting-drinking-next -18-years-ellen-degeneres/2642578002/.

11. Kristian Stanfill, Instagram post, November 9, 2022, https://www.instagram .com/p/Ckv1MFNpJcA/.

CHAPTER 20: ANTICIPATE DEATHBED REGRETS

1. Billy Graham, *Just As I Am: The Autobiography of Billy Graham* (San Francisco: HarperOne, 1997).

2. Nelson Mandela, *Long Walk to Freedom* (Boston: Little, Brown and Company, 1994), Chapter 109.

3. Nelson Mandela, *Long Walk to Freedom*.

4. Billy Graham, *Just As I Am*.

Chapter 22: The Wisest Decision Anyone Can Make

1. Blaise Pascal, "Pascal's Wager," in *Pensées* (1660).
2. C. S. Lewis, *The Joyful Christian: 127 Readings* (New York: Scribner, 1996).
3. Max Lucado, *He Chose the Nails: What God Did to Win Your Heart* (Nashville, TN: Thomas Nelson, 2017).

Chapter 23: Practicing Gratitude

1. Dietrich Bonhoeffer, *Letters and Papers from Prison* (New York: Simon & Schuster, 1953).
2. Michael Craig Miller, MD, "In Praise of Gratitude," Harvard Health Publishing, November 21, 2012, https://www.health.harvard.edu/blog/in-praise-of-gratitude-201211215561.
3. G. K. Chesterton, *A Short History of England* (London, Chatto & Windus, 1917).
4. Meister Eckhart (1260–1327) quote, Goodreads, https://www.goodreads.com/quotes/15189-if-the-only-prayer-you-said-was-thank-you-that.

Chapter 24: Finishing Well

1. John Piper, "It Is the Spirit That Gives Life," Desiring God, December 13, 2009, https://www.desiringgod.org/messages/it-is-the-spirit-that-gives-life.
2. C. S. Lewis, *Mere Christianity* (New York: HarperOne, 2001), 28.

About the Author

 Mark DeMoss is a public relations practitioner, executive, and consultant of four decades—nearly three of them as president of DeMoss, the firm he founded and ran from 1991–2019 to serve faith-based organizations and causes. Several hundred nonprofit organizations, corporations, and leaders have sought counsel and support from him in communications, media relations, branding, marketing, nonprofit management, and crisis management. Mark and his wife, April, live in the Atlanta area. They have three grown children and are expecting their sixth grandchild.